Fluttertongue 5

Other Books by Steven Ross Smith

Poetry:
Fluttertongue 4: Adagio for the Pressured Surround, NeWest Press, 2007
Fluttertongue 3: disarray, Turnstone Press, 2005
Transient Light, Mercury Press, 1990
Blind Zone, Aya Press (Mercury), 1985

Fiction:
Lures, Mercury Press, 1997

Non-fiction:
Celebrating Saskatchewan Artists, Saskatchewan Arts Alliance, 2007
Ballet of the Speech Organs: Bob Cobbing on Bob Cobbing, as interviewed by
Steven Ross Smith. Underwhich Editions, 1998.

Fluttertongue 5

Everything Appears To Shine With Mossy Splendour

Steven Ross Smith

TURNSTONE PRESS

Fluttertongue 5
Everything Appears To Shine With Mossy Splendour
copyright © Steven Ross Smith 2011

Turnstone Press
Artspace Building
206-100 Arthur Street
Winnipeg, MB
R3B 1H3 Canada
www.TurnstonePress.com

Turnstone Press gratefully acknowledges the assistance of the Canada Council for the Arts, the Manitoba Arts Council, the Government of Canada through the Canada Book Fund, and the Province of Manitoba through the Book Publishing Tax Credit and the Book Publisher Marketing Assistance Program.

Phrases from *Turneresque*, are copyright © Elizabeth Willis, Burning Deck, Providence, RI, 2003. Used by permission. Phrases from *Meteoric Flowers*, are copyright © Elizabeth Willis, Wesleyan University Press, Middletown, CT, 2006. Used by permission.

Cover design: Jamis Paulson
Interior design: Sharon Caseburg
Printed and bound in Canada by Friesens for Turnstone Press.

Library and Archives Canada Cataloguing in Publication

Smith, Steven, 1945–
    Fluttertongue 5 : everything appears to shine with
mossy splendour / Steven Ross Smith.

Poems.
ISBN 978-0-88801-378-1

    I. Title. II. Title: Fluttertongue five. III. Title: Everything appears to shine with mossy splendour.

PS8587.M59F585 2011   C811'.54   C2011-902366-0

Contents

Generations have trod, have trod, have trod;
And all is seared with trade; Bleared, smeared with toil;
And wears man's smudge and shares man's smell: the soil
Is bare now, nor can foot feel, being shod.

—Gerard Manley Hopkins (from *God's Grandeur*)

Fluttertongue 5

The sperm of mosses is biflagellate, i.e. they have two flagellae that aid in propulsion. Since the sperm must swim to the archegonium, fertilization cannot occur without water.

In some mosses, green vegetative structures called gemmae are produced on leaves or branches, which can break off and form new plants without the need to go through the cycle of fertilization.

—Wikipedia

A Fly In The Keyhole

What a buzz! Cellophane flicker a vibrato of panic. Musca domestica as key or peg. A magic turn in a passage meant for entry. Tarnished brass and metal smell of time and conjunction. A vagina opens to a penis that enters like a cotter locking on love. Yesterday was different. Castles were burning to the hum of vibrating cell phones. His dental work was prolonged, the mould set hard too soon. There is always something wrong in the world. Tumblers are not tripped by currents of air. Though this night it turns possible. A black fly spits on its food to liquefy it, to make it easy to swallow. Moans fill the room, sharp cries between pants. Imagine, to taste and smell with the hairs on your legs.

Black Rock Moss . Andreaèa Rupestris
You! Tall one with cell (sell) phone
phosphorescent and demanding

Standing By The Boat

Slaps you hear, an aria of summer. Soft laps, evocative against the hull. Love once made its name there, moist on the prow. A bobbing mast. A furrow in the damp sand. A masterful painting that captures Eros and Translucence. Sweet and salty. Elvis's iconic swivelly hips speak of peppery innocence. Near the equator. Honest to godliness. Palm trees and string-thing bathing suits gasp news flashes with a biting tang. You can hear the flip-flop, or is that the flap of the wind-lashed sail? A tsunami of pelvises. Gentlemen prefer bonds and on the prowl will ogle. Roots auburn and tentative on a tide-kissed beach.

with wide screens **screaming**
bend to the **pubic** adherent *Andreaea*
her black and dark-reddish **tufts**, when moist

Deceptions Of Nocturnal Hair

Coiffed or askew. Strands to live by in a world of quick judgment. Revealed when the door opens, the skirt hikes up and the bulbs go off. The collapse of globular clusters is worrisome. With a certain decorum or disguise and a flash. Dog owners seem less so in agility classes. Bit off more than he could cherish. Verbs vanish from the dictionary page even in a dogged search, a splitting of hairs. When wet, a Superbowl of spores. Let your fall be pillowed. "A halo of sultry slate" he called hers, late that evening. "Spiky grapple" was his in the morning. Seconds to go in the daily clutch though time may not exist as a watch-hand moves and a physicist cannot prove otherwise. A toothy brush combs ecstasy, itself a wave and beyond the game. Dances in the pocket, cocked.

widely spreading, her sporophytes raised on short stalks
her capsules black, shaped like footballs
—appeal to grappling tackles and long and deep—

More Lovely Than The Ash

The laden world. The ladled word. A scooper and a bucket to hold the dead heat. Luck be a labile night. How to mean beauty? The rattle and scuff of heavy rock rocks thought right off the page. And beauty from the stage. Grey and crumbled, it flies up at a breath, speaks of what was, spins what's seen, and tickles a nose like bubbly wine but much drier. Toast with the black scraped off. Old skin and a blood blister. Beside a lamb, a child stands on a bomb. *Guess what* is a trick question applied to some body parts. No gestures of powder and blush, but something intrinsic, inexplicable, unbuyable. A chunk of skull over there. Right here, the downy hairs that tail just below the navel.

or shaped like spindles (she'd prefer, as would you, her yarded wool).
Beneath—and to which she clings—
is dry acid rock. Acid rock. Granitic or psychedelic

Basket With Crashing Birds

Small and white—Gertrude's dog. A weave of willow-thought, red and dry in the plains' parched air. The cursor hints at italic. Flitting fowl not so much weft as frenzy. Casualties quilted and clustered at rest, the bereft fingering. Yesterday the sky had the clarity of lemon. Today, pomegranate, blood-red. Think about Picasso—would he, attending Gertrude's salon, bend to pet the yappy fur-ball snapping at his cuff? Or lift a feather? Back to the matter of fact, of fancy. Of lines given in a theatre of sleep and strings of drool from corners of mouths in nodding heads. Where's the fiery prod, wings that creak, the sting of tragedy's truth? Quadrupeds are colour-blind, or perhaps not. What deception claims the crafty crow? The proscenium in which it all plays out, inverts to a cradle's curve, a coffin's ornament, an overture's soar that becomes a wailing ache. Praise and grace are stomped before the vast expanse of invisible sad glass.

(Jimi or Grace) Slick that is, and Hendrix.
A voice **hums** its animal age with White Rabbit, Foxy Lady
(hymns to **mosses'** underfootedness) and **zones**

A Mirror Of Temporary

Someone you recognize stares back. Certain teas are promoted as cure-alls and preventives against the bugs that march through. So easy to find spiritual teaching if you're on the lookout. Blues brothers and soul sisters sing. Sip and you will know. It appears that the soul can be glimpsed in a mirror held over a shoulder in candlelight, but only in a flash, and if there's no mirror-error. Though desirable, is it necessary to state the truth? The saintly face, a glimpse, a moment ago. A reader might not search a zoo for a novel though cages are filled with characters and tigers roar between flipped pages on more than one occasion. The assembly of text on a page is a scan of your brain structure at any given moment. Monks sit sangha. References to time pass before you without your awareness of the wisp of a breeze that carries a flake of you away. Channels grow in relation to stimuli. Time to pray for the safe journey of the soul of James Brown, that awaits departure on flashy dancing feet on the rear platform of the last car of the night train. Divert your eyes from the glass or track to lift your cup and it's out of sight in a flash with a flutter and a mewl.

back to a **lava** lamp and traffic lights pulsing to primal **rhythm** and a stone stoned candle holder that **melts and reforms** with plasticene pliancy. *Andreaea* moist and

Goo Or Folding

On my forehead ... on my typewriter, said the poet Hannah Weiner, of words that entered her field of vision out of nowhere. Special delivery in questionable atmospheric conditions. A blizzard outside creates a million surfaces of flake, each one a screen that captures light that holds a word in its wavelength. Scuff of shovels and pens. Slivered those words right into her poems. Ploughs scrape through eventually and a degree of levelness is gained. Imagine, some languages have no word for *snowplough.* Some, no word for *shootout,* though bullets fly through walls and foreheads everywhere. Words stuck in the air like stars, messages from God's projector, words the lips strain to pull from the frontal lobe, to kiss, to articulate. Poets would pay for that. Mystics and shamans appear quaint nowadays but the search is on in mosh pits and clusters of birdwatchers. Huge black wheels and thick treads gum up the roads. Street signs and maps, seen even in a daze, pretend order. We're wild inside and the map defies the fold's embrace.

widely spreading. See **blackness** between red beats.
Black and dark red she is. *Andreaea*'s leaves can be round or **star-shaped**
—embrace of earth and **night** sky—

Lantern, Honey

Somewhere, between west and wild, light dims as the setting sun winks over lodgepole-pine-covered hills. Black needles spike down the dark as a flick of wrist and scritch of a match fill the room with amber glow. The pages of the book speak of hard and soft, of time and space and oneness. With a buzz. Earlier a wiper blade went rigid, snapped in the frigid wind. "Worst winter I can remember." Oh so sweet, the scent between her legs. So sombre as he signs the petition to stop the war, just as, on the other side of the world, shrapnel enters the groin of an innocent. Does weather have its plans for you … or does God? It was on the trip to the post office, everything iced up. A letter mailed, full of regret and churlish motivation, like bad bathroom manners, or probing an electrical outlet for residue with a nail. Toothpicks were once made not from slivers of wood but from the bones of small animals. *I'm standing in line waiting for a ticket to my passing.* As his forehead grows cold, he wishes the touch of her warm tongue there. Ah yes, he remembers, vividly, that moment, its innocence, its flickering light sticky in his hands—was it nectar, was it blood?

The tall **one's** made smaller
Small enough to **writhe with** tough
lust at black-rock-moss-**touch**.

The Bleeding Ankle

It was the time of the end of safety, but not the first time, not the first end. So hard to concentrate in the persistent chill and the wind-down groan of failing batteries, of contusion. Cherish was not something to consider in the heart's conflict, in the holding on. With every bounce a rubber ball lands on a different surface. Biography is a vein that is not what it seams. The subway leads to inferno, burns high, burns low. A certain group of poets cannot convene or compose because of snow and trepidation. The imagery in certain poems can only be written in particular regions. Take snow for instance, or blood blushing the bare foot. Inevitable horror. Brando in shadows. Sadness caps the conversation. Something not foreseen, its soft tragedy. *Repetition* is essential to the dancer who feels the pattern in his feet, or learning Latin, though Stein calls it *insistence*. Exposed bone, reveal of tendon, reveal of nerve, the underpin.

Andreaea's grace less slick than persistent, is
tenacious and tough to remove.

Common Haircap Moss . Polytrichum Commune

Forever Won't Survive

The voices speak in absolutes, abstractions, with a warble, a high pitch and all at once. A case to be made or hoisted to the overhead bin. A bloodied fist pounds a table in resistance. Wintering sparrows puff up skyward like an explosion of drier lint, or like birds puffing to the sky. A chest pops open, its heart extracted in a fist. How long is time or an organ donor's moment? What serrated blade's just gone by? Pencils at work. A rough path leads through it. Orange, its skin pocked yet shiny as almost always. Devilish. He wonders where the wild is as the frozen car keeps him from the fish market. The wish market, its timeless salty whiff. Everything appears to be exterior, a validation of surfaces, thought is thought to be illusion. A scalpel or a scythe's dark glint at the corner of your eye, uninvited, bites.

One single alphabetic strophe at the top of its midrib tier, shaped
U, with edges, coarsely-toothed.
Each one (the one, not the tooth) is unisexual.

14

Declare It Thinly

Razored into skin, a word, a whim, a ticket to fate. Jingle jangle electronic cacophony. The Beats *beat* it nation-wide, samadhi, satori, with beatific smiles and whoever turns their pages holds in hands the blessèd or blistering steering wheel and spins it like an arcade game in blazing sun or teeming starlight. Late last night, steam from the river could have frozen lungs. Poem, driven through—its air so slight, barely a bump, a ripple. After all, it's twenty-four-seven of hoods, hounds, and Hollywood, all video titillation. Starlets slim as toffee drawn through straws. The plug popped and stopped the car, despite the biceps' bulge. Jack declared, in Chorus 196, *Wanta bring everyone straight to the dream*, and he did—loaded a generation into his typewriter and hit the keys spontaneous, somnambulant. Tingling skin, all there is between arousal and nothingness. Time's slim ribbon runs through slimmer space. Where is radiance? Leaders with fat ambition and anorexic minds build walls and fences or crater them. Everyone abides the drought and steps up for the rain dance. The privileged race that likes to live a cut or two above its station to escape the cloacal trenches. It seems slo-mo, but it's a skinny minute as we drop toward the blade, each sleek side on offer—grace or grit ... and oh, the turbulent gyrations.

This Ulysses robust, dark green
with enlarged head at the tip
in arousal, constant.

They Seem To Be Loving Us

Let's not kid—there's a longing for youth, as age sets in, in the drive-thru lane of Life. No-man's-land is a place where men are drawn in numbers to stake a claim. Shooting pains in the shoulder wake us when we want comfort and sleep. A cell phone gives life a direction, a strange public voice. "You have limitless love," says the small boy. Flood from a busted sprinkler line stains the day's envelope. A kiss there, a stroke here, is who we remember. Man's land cluttered with cluster-cut, cluster-bomb, claustrophobia, clitorectomy, circumcision, colonoscopy, clot, collateral damage. Gloomy predictions overwhelm states of grace. *Cranky* is a word and a demeanour that sounds like a piston in need of lubricant but what is the fluid that opens the heart? Search for the connection of each one in the mire that hides rays of light. Hard to escape the tone of a title. Who are *They? Us?* Blessèd are pine grosbeaks, so trusting at the winter seed cache, so vulnerable in crimson, grey and yellow garb, so soft and unassuming in their beauty.

While Anna Livia **sports** her usual sporophytes. From **spores** come more stems and leaves—**and sex organs.** In the woods, bracken ferns are brown, fallen, but their rhizomes are **spread**ing

Match Not Struck

Late or latent. Incendiary force bound in red and blue. It's a playoff, local brain power versus the chain of life. A question of the letter g. Forlorn whiff in the air. A purloined host's heavenly antibody. Crispness melts on the tongue like latte foam or smoke. Sun glares. City, quiet, snared in snow and sparse of cars. Postponement of the versus game. The outdoor network, once upon a time, was not on television. Beauty of a face bathed in brittle pixel-light in a studio of screens and forgotten steroidal ignition. The Interac machine withholds its keyboard. An arsonist's art doubles him over his knees with heartburn. Paramedics drive with an air of calm, even with a siren blaring, brighter than a flame.

well below the mosses. That croak
—frog or bird? Or Bob Dylan's brittle throat—sings far above hunkering
moss that loves the wetness of the forest floor.

In Terror Surely

Purchase carbon credits for avoidance. *Om* and *asana* for serenity and strength, reaching while not reaching for *samadhi*. The place of crumbling towers now with inescapable dark echo of what's beyond silence, even amidst the throb of daily pulse and resurrection. Hustle of feet and swinging doors. Beggars stretch hands and hats for change. On the thirty-third floor, workers turn the wheels of commerce and trade, and occasionally glance through the huge expanse of glass toward the imperial sky. Debate heats up—the faster the atmosphere, the cooler the action. Footing less sure day by day. Looking for a setting to inspire? The customer enters from the street and the smile from the young blue-eyed bank teller melts coins in his palm to feed the bank's bottom line. What can be spared? Separate self from other selves. In the off-leash grounds, arched branches, white with soufflé poufs of snow, bow to make a tunnel of wowing beauty that crouches the adventurer, she who wishes to stay forever, but must pass through. Ancestors conserved until war taught them to consume for comfort. How to share, with the world, a plateful of salad and squash?

Haircap thrives in dryness—there, just to confuse, all (whichever sex) are lance-shaped, thrusting from a membranous, sheathed base. These lusty mosses, spears at ready, their trade of pronominal referents,

Singed Paper On The Stoop

Chocolate and *tariff* on the tongue in the spelling bee. Sweetness and the fee, all nerves and twitter. Cogwheel in the stomach and tongue-twist to protect. Heave of furniture down the steps, top to bottom. A face burns with failure (or success), a chest fills with sorrow. *Illicit* trips a tongue. An empty crate dumped in an alley waits for someone to try to make a home out of strife. Illumination or elimination. Steps lead up and down, but which is over it. She paces the classroom after a long absence, her thoughts singed and distracted by illicit love. *Curriculum*, the rattle, the riddle. On the dotted line. On the last step, down from the porch, half-buried in snow, a diamond earring gleams—the brightest crystal. Can love be that simple . . . that hard to find? Charred at edges and stooped to loss—sadness casts its spell, slumps each one to the lowlands.

sex organs charged with
mossiness. And always
topped with a showy hat.

19

A Dime In Private

A round question. An accord sung, a wrapper, a roll and a census in a rare application. A decade of spare change. The dolorous, let them gather. Is it more worthy to keep to self than to enter the exchange? Glinting, dated, embossed with a royal head. A gleam, a rare chance, a lock on decreasing value, or gain. The cyber-sex he had on the Internet with a nineteen-year-old just happened, he told his wife. *She seemed interested in me—she has hair like yours.* Through the ceiling-mounted speakers, a lilt, a lingering aria in soprano, possibly reaching high C. Light bulbs burn out, plunge rooms into caverns of shadows forming and lost. Reader, please note—words here have been deleted and will never be known. If lost before knowing, not missed? Words formed in the dark—spoken or not—compel, seem larger, but may be illusory, even if expressions of love. The anger beneath reason will shatter trust and erupt and propel, like file-sharpened razor-edged coins rocketed by a Semtex explosion. "A cyber babe shamed me—he's not worth a dime—I'm shaving my head—I'm going shopping—chicken breasts, even on sale, add up," she said, all in the same breath.

Large **Hair** *Moss . Oligotrichum* **parallelum**
That application of adjective to the nearest noun **means**
hair is large, not moss, per se. Moss, **despite itself,**

My Mental Fence

Did you read it or dread it? The day's busyness, its conflicts, make the mind go faster than running feet or hands and *fight or flight* pounds in the chest. Blossoms are sought by the eye at the crossroads though petals resist a grasp and none grow near the razor-wire. A smoky yet excellent book crosses the palm of the event organizer with an acrid plume. She said no to skating and iced a heart. Cigarettes are making a comeback in the movies. A gift of sixteen chocolates, light and dark, mouth-watering in each case, and apparently good for endorphin release if eaten with restraint or a lover, will help the cause. Introductions must be prepared, to seem spontaneous. A feeling of sorrow embedded around the eyes, and despite pretense, transmitted through skin. Difficult to lock the chest and keep an open heart. The bank drags its feet and sacks of money when it's time to relinquish some to the rightful owner. Snow in a boot makes a boy, leaning on a post and shaking a foot, cry and curse those boots as only an eleven year old can. An icy wind filled with dogs baring teeth. Sunset between the buildings viewed while leaning on the bridge rail casts a melancholy light on faces there, though laughter had earlier bloomed. The two-foldedness of hinged seconds.

by its hair, harkens
to the sixties, the 1960s. Nobody under
fifty has had the thrill of Jimi Hendrix live, his smokin' guitar

Nature Leans Away

Perhaps in self-protection. A guardedness. Trees there, a sly caution, an old photograph. Value is auctionable to their detriment. Gnarly branches of beauty. Cymbals sting the air, syntax rolls from lips. A sneeze threatens to break out, prompts a pair of fingers to rush up, press the nostril closed. Hockey stars worshipped as national heroes. So far away we've moved from understanding the turn of a blade of brome grass. Left or right, no matter, closed in from all sides. Unable to find the environmental comment on the editorial page he mourns two losses, knows it will be too late when the time is right. Winter follows the traveller with its densely packed snow. *Would you like your balance?* The canal will likely be frozen over. Triumph will occur, but with an outcome different than imagined. Blind to evanescence.

or Michael Bloomfield or Sly. But
the magic of image capture has kept their haloing
hair alive, though now appears quaint. No thick moss, no

This Idyll We'd Be

To gaze upon its itness—a diaphanous lush garden, or a night river twinkling with reflected light—creates nostalgic longing, even in those who've never known such a scene. Truly, a hip cannot be replaced, a memory's catalyst reactivated. An organism yearns. Peanut butter is so good—the lover licks the last bits from his teeth, then returns to the jar with a knife, a sticky kiss. Polanski has a way with an image. This is an understatement. A ringing phone goes unanswered. Shuffling down the walkway to board the aircraft, a flyer becomes intimate with the back of a stranger's neck. One imagines a certain languid, perhaps lost, quality. Repairs build up to a point of obsolescence. Purchase the DVD and study the digital eloquence to enter a wild and beautiful mind, tinged with darkness. As she emerges from the lake, on her bare shoulders droplets luminous and compelling enliven her flesh and conduct the viewer's erotic dream. A new car excites, but won't replace love. The desire to lick again. A plenitude of surgeries to fix things up incises loss.

rich green slowly-spreading loose mats hold a lens' attention,
because mosses have underdeveloped
water- and food-conducting systems, and so seem dormant when dry.

This Alias Stands

Lime green colour is not often chosen, though seems to be making a comeback in clothing and accessories. The postwoman shuffles letters. As a writer reaches for a pen a quiver unsettles his belly and seems, above it, to push tears from nowhere, to trickle over the lid and down his cheek. Crisper than usual. Can these costumed words be trusted with all the corruption in Hollywood and Fort McMurray? The long-time trusty vehicle is headed for the rusty graveyard or the auto auction. A question of capital. Long and shapely legs in the crosswalk. Top Forty this, Top Ten that. A helpful and congenial serviceman fosters loyalty. They're all in the same boast where there's standing room only with benefit to the towering. Authors gather a locus of generosity. Still shaky, he tries to discover who he is at the bottom of his nature. The young and hip walk with a certain rocking motion, as do the aged, but so different, so hip conscious. A clean sweep on the colourful track, the parade of masquerade.

When moss is re-wetted, **photosynthesis** cranks up immediately, **makes sugar and oxygen** and enriching greenness. A new costume and the **return** of big hair. Come

A Piece Of Glass

Entering a time of zero tolerance and sub-zero temperatures. The peace march is in the streets and on the Internet where protesters walk with fingers. That cold virus returns like a loyal friend, its familiar catarrh. A jagged edge catches the sun like a barbed remark from a lover and increases pain. The trouble with technology is we made it but it's not like anyone we know yet does things for us while extending our bodies and our minds beyond ourselves. Meeting and obligation flux in the daybook's day. Always an impending breakdown or unturned page—have you had your service check, your expectations validated, your bi-focal focused? The mystery of the spectrum and realization of sight's limitations. Perhaps the acid-heads were right. Particles are always accelerating, pieces of art in themselves, *we are stardust.* Icicles form beneath the car body's mobile cave. Mister Prime Minister addresses the nation with the usual murky profusion of platitudes, of prevarication, of penetralia. The pet dog has a condition and so does her master whom she resembles, their pug faces, their bowed walks. Silver-blue and convex. Nobody feels healthy anymore.

to **think** of it, it rained at Woodstock. But it's **mud**
we **remember**, not moss.
But don't think moss isn't rockin'. A drifting single-celled **moss** spore

Said The Box

Talk talk talk through a forehead sluggish with mugs. Who needs this? It's a burden to care. Is an email apology an apology? The car has a sun-roof and through it see grey clouds and droplets of incessant rain that ripple and run. It heats up, though many seem to doubt. Not happy with the way things are going in the land of promises and hopes. *Be concrete,* the teacher often said, *and think outside cliché.* Like a knife warmed under tapwater then moved to the pale yellow cube to slice through it like a knife slices butter, not a trowel in the slurry. The ceramic heater belts it out. So do Etta James and Ruthie Foster. Twilight and satellite. God is a tripped relay. One had three wives alive, and the other three ones dead— *coffined,* you might say. The conference will be about science and healing and poetry, not synonymous but woven.

lands on a **wet** branch and germinates, producing
a shoot or gametophyte—**and sure** enough,
on that small **gamey** stem, sex organs—male and female—appear and

Rustling In Gauze

Gazelle or ghazal. Someone will justify the finances of a lab for the study of anomalies. The shape of antibodies. Generate against the virus. Icagel your constantly moving and germ-laden hands. Jazz'll get your knee knocking. Everyone uses lip-balm to be kissable, wants to explode with a lover. Blondness isn't everything, but attracts, with a degree of tolerance for the lingering scent of the colour treatment, the sales of which have reached new levels, and surely started with the tresses of Marilyn Monroe, her puckered lips and the up-ruffle of her skirt. The young couple do their homework every day in the café with occasional tender eyes across the table, neither being blond, but the headiness of Psych 101 and touching knees. His earphones are a California dreamin' crown. The white and blue Tyvek not sealed by red tape flutters in the winter breeze, lifts and drops with a plastic-flap-crackle against the wall of the unfinished building in Saskatoon where a workman slips on a wet board and plunges one short storey. It's a fiction, a fissionable universe. The elegant animal finds itself leaping in poetic form. Such a soft sound, fingers rubbing beside an ear, perhaps thunder to a bat. Or a battalion advancing by stealth in the fabric of the dark.

begin to get it on, producing sperm and eggs. And where does the sperm head (so to speak)? For—where else?—the egg, to fertilize! Next,

Swing Like Faces

A hand, knuckles turning white, in one scene, grips and soars, in another grips the handle and pours wonderful brown liquid heat into a mug. Lift, tilt, sip, turn. Waiting for a head of spiky hair. The professor at the window-counter-seat looks down in concentration, white hair wisped across his brow, thought-lost, his black pen scripting white pages. Drive the scrubbed station wagon to the auto auction lot, push the door against the cold-wind-blast-shudder that rocks the car, frosts the eyelids of the bidders. On book back covers people say the kindest things. A world where a voice can raise hairs in places you don't often think of, like your wrist, your nape, your eyebrows, or Bogotá. An unfamiliar face that's familiar. Back and forth and a fifth down the hatch, expecting to be disappointed or improved. White knuckle on a link of chain. Another phrase escapes along a tractor track, a gorgeous geometric pattern in the soil softened slightly by a gentle passing rain. The sound of a singing voice, an echo along the pew, hovers in a quiet pause. What was her name from a long way back, the toothy stalker? Glee in a child's eyes flung through space and a squeal. Mozart's concertos are always in the air—a tilt might find one.

from the **gametophyte**, grows a **sporophyte**, a capsule on a stalk—capsule with teeth (purpose unknown). The capsule releases spores to **start the** cycle over again. It's a quiet non-stop **orgy**

The Digitized Chandelier

Bared or barbed. A bee, a bonny visage, light spilt from overhead. Real or virtual, the shot pans from the dining room to the swimming pool beside the ocean in Mexico where a cerebral cortex dreams in primary colours. Or is that the hippocampus, college jokes of heavy mammals notwithstanding? The hardware salesman sprinkles chocolate on his latte foam. Blond streaks in dark shaggy hair and a nose ring that needs a Kleenex and a cheesy lyric and conducts cold to a tender membrane. Crystal drugs and a knife through cellophane and a pitted gleam. "We're in hot water or a corrupted PDF file." What price in the decor terminal? A life takes its life. Anguish in a mother's eyes, hands, soles of her feet. A tray a portrait a chocolate parfait a dissemblage a buzz and crumbled nose, all tissue, metal, and glass in their semblance. A piercing cry, death rattle depth-charge dispossession depression distressed de-essence of a dispirited spirit. Someone, please lift us up like spiky wheat heads ripened in high plains sun. Beneath faceted glitter, a bubble rises in the fluted champagne glass, but once.

—don't think an isolated incident—it's a
rave, a never-ending mosh-pit with nine thousand species of moss
sprinkled all over the world. And you didn't notice.

Two Upon The Dew

Opposite of metal. Scar on his face traced by the mineral alchemy of drying droplets. The music a skronk, a tinny abstraction that scratches like a backward play. Beneath the proscenium the family's despair. Torn through their minds like a pair of coyotes that lope across the prairie morning's tawny grasses, freeze the edge of the bush, and look back at the automobile busting up the road. A flower brown and poked through snow-dust. Music creaks through woofers. The wine is Spanish and spicy, but smooth. Everyone, speaking French or English or an indiscernible language—a cacophony suddenly stops, as eyes turn to the fireplace to gaze in silence and deep listening. The Swiss Army knife offers a magnifying glass to enable the squinter to study a map or a bill or these words. A scroll in Japanese calligraphy is uninterpretable by those present, but beautiful nontheless The multicultural typist has spastic fingers. Fire blazes the exquisitely built log pyramid, and nearby is the evidence, the only sign of the body's struggle, a reddish complexion and powder-blue toque of fabulous cable knit, and *parlez* that carries on. How can a word replace the injured, the hoping-to-recover human spirit? It's more than can be dug in the heart's pit—gravel or blood.

Here on—watch for the big hair.

Crane's Bill Moss . Atrichum selwynii
Crane to see the crane's bill (little for

Anything But Twilight

Faster than a speeding bullet they said of the Man of Steel—but could
have been that big hare bounding, tearing up the field toward the darker
edge. A lilty chant to Krishna on the temple-plain. It's warm for winter,
so the walker unzips, opens his coat across his chest. Television gives
each tongue a common syntax, and each hour a disappointing spin. But
tomorrow there'll be a levy on the heat of the sun which will rise with
emissions and election fever. Definitely faster than a heart-patient's feet
on a treadmill in a stress-test and the cardiogram needle's twitchy dance.
Viral outbreak in the shiny health centre, floors polished to a gleam,
sterile stents and archaic stenographic machines, draft in the vent. But the
whole world is scientific and is scared and is washing its hands. Ginkgo
leaf, sacred. Tiny rodent tracks across snow just at the edge of the stony
bed the river left behind in its quest for less resistance. The waters rush,
make you think of a fair maiden's gusted hair, her gusseted waist. In the
distance lace curtains part to cling to fading daylight. Lips zipped open
by the chinook and with much to say. Biota on the march. The gravel
machine, a huge green monster with rumbling skin and snout, hovers in
the pit's crease at the margin of sight, leans into the fold, recedes into a
shadow's grip.

comparison on Pacific's coast, the
Sandhill being rare). Leaves shaped
like a **lance** or **tongue**—(pierce with a **word** or **jab**)—and pointed

31

Rifle, If Lucy

A flock of golden-eye rises from the river on rapid wings and begins its soft trilling flight upstream startled by the upright man and his sniper potential, though unarmed. She runs the panelogic channel, gabs over coffee, runs her fingers through her red hair on black and white TV. BB King chooses the formal form of address for his guitar, but he's a class act. Lucid. It's all entertainment and a bit of wit. Thrill is on the wing-rise. The show goes on despite itself, cartoon or cartoonish. The river dips beneath ice and resurfaces downstream with more force, but creates a backwater where ducks hover anew, dive and preen, a cabaret in black and white with gem-eyes. A name with light. Survival instinct on wing. An aim and an explosion, quaint. A right and *goddamm if I'll conform—there's thugs out there*. In the play it was the shots not heard that took the engineering women and the aftershock that took survivors down. He could duck but he could not hide. The dial is loose, broken, the air rife with fear. A stark, sharp note.

For all this aggression, *A. selwynii* seems **ambivalent**—
hunkers down in **loose** mats at stream
edges and **on** soil-covered rock **ledges**—though a bit of **a daredevil**—

Fever, An Alcove

Against torpor a need to rise though a grey weight sits poultice-heavy on the sleeper so feeds recurrent slumber. Every morning life's incunabula. A bill is sent for the crucible's recovery. Trembling, furnaced, the body puts up a fight. Dial-up technology thwarts the seeker, dove-coloured cuffs at his wrists. Poets are evoked for spirit, sensitivity in a chattery room whose bar is closing, or in a real estate ad selling lofts. A recipe for the delicious cumin bread is savoury potential. There's more though, to see—the not-loved, the loved-but-kept-away, the loved-of-a-kind—more words in the Thesaurus, but they'll have to make their own combinations, the honking vees of migrating geese, or squealy freight-train cars where whines ratchet, ricochet, pain in the couplings. Each one a customer cornered in the cup of a cell phone, switched to India, to a call-centre voice that bewilders. Whether to reach for *The Bible* or *The Yoga Sutras of Patanjali* to guide—or *Slaughterhouse Five*? A line to copy in the fray-edged notebook which contains all the words of passing and hope-to-hold. Frustration and hopelessness itch, while a worthy possibility disorients like metal stacking chairs, unstacked and scattered at the icy edge by the river's flow. *All pavilions a-flutter,* writes John Ashbery. Shake down the mercury and turn it in to the pharmacy, the world's gone digital. Chill, get a degree for happiness before the security pat-down's thorough caress.

And that **kru-ru-u-u** call will not guide you to moss
But to a rare sighting of its **avian** namesake.

*Cord Moss . Fun**aria** hygrometrica*

33

Her Cheek Of Luxe

A pleasure, aroused in the mind's privacy, dwarfs that mind, fills the room. Light blooms, shreds the walls, even to closed eyes. Soft and round the subtlest hill, or a peach just ripe and rose-buffed, felt in the loin. The gravel truck snorts down the road kicking dust, gusty tail spreading, chuffing over the split-rail fence that offers no protection. Sprays enough to scrim Eros' invisible pulse into oblivion. Brown grasses in winter huff out their air and lie down to wait though some will rise no more. Turn of phrase without a signal-flicker. It's his shoulder, just below the blade he remembers, her softness there, her lips there. Fever and writhe. Abuse of the apostrophe. A cruise ship fills with fans of poetry who cheer on free verse, internal rhyme, parsing and parsley, disjunctive sage-thought, sonority, pinot noir, the iamb of God, haiku with sake, and a stop at every poet's port even if an island or inland or interred. What a lark, a meadow full! What a fan dance!! He can't turn away as the shoulder aches its loss. A fruit of palest yellow, its droplets at the corner of his mouth.

Now let's talk character—moss as weed? Moss
as contortionist. At that, with yellow parts
amidst the green and

A Cup May Be A Sword

A tourist is a receptacle or a prod. *We are born as verbs rather than nouns,* says Agnes Martin. The sixty-five year old Canadian grandma walking in Mexico City is mugged and aims her knee for his crotch but misses and he yanks her purse away. Thrust and receive in a union of opposites. A slender one opens her arms and cups a suitor's head, while stabbing her love into his heart, minutes after the balcony, and somewhere, of course, music plays. A smooth rose-coloured pebble that slips through a dark pocket's worn gap. A painter in a quaint corner of Saskatchewan lifts passion in a brushstroke, though jabbed by business, a virus and a need to articulate on canvas an image of existence, of reverence, in oils, carefully crafted and rendered with authentic resonance, though interpretive, and the swashbuckle most subtle. Oh beloved, the heart's denial, a blade-glint born of necessity. Absence packs a daily dream. Phone call to mom and the boy feels in balance though a broken wrist will not heal in an instant. A book recommended, one spirit to another. Sweetheart in the justified lines. Balls she thrust for and screamed the anger and loss from her whole life. Burn of concern miles away over Portuguese wine and a curry meal. The fireplace glows, the underburn of logs, an orange slash on gazing eyes, and the body receives and gives its heat.

decorated like a fruit tree with pear-
shaped hanging capsules. A weed
that takes to disturbed soil that's packed down and loaded

A Boy Among Crows

Cold out there, a matter of black and white. They've flown south and he is east of here. Speaking of the winged ones and a young son. Mad-seeming verse can land you in the asylum, ask Pound, ask Clare. The lamp has a shade of hide, stitched and bound in an authentic way and is pale and scarred. Pause to lick an envelope the colour of a golden Lab that waits at its master's feet. The squeals and caws, notes heard from yesterdays ago. Elemental, and burning, like an Ani DiFranco protest song or the fado of Argentina Santos. Strikes the core between the heart and gut. In spring the corvid conversations will return gawky syntax to neighbourhood trees and sound like argument and love. A young man will boot the white and black soccer ball against the wooden fence, over and over and over, sharp-soft smack of leather on wood—smack-thump, thud. Repetition is a sign of life and life repeats itself again and again, but only once in the grand scheme—reincarnation notwithstanding—though who knows for sure? Wail and rile, caws in the copse. The poets locked between the notes still scribble and mark up the page—their pencils hover and swirl, dive-bomb the fault looking for a quake. Thump, thump, thump, a boot against the limits.

with nitrogen from cows or deer or people—that's right: **flap, patty, scat or crap**—note the common flat 'a'. And even **shat** and seeks fire's after-after-glow, settling in when flame's **passed** through

Something Less Lovely

Ticked and tickle. A feather under the nose. Snuggling down again after tea warms the throat and the rack of the world that quarters citizens in pain, that stretches, snaps striations that underline the skin, drifts in, interrupts sumptuous lunch and afternoon slumber. Guitar strings initiate escape in the mind's ear, the drum's inf(l)ection. Always the pursuit of beauty stumbles at the brink, too late the flip-switch that trips the dozed-off aperture at the site of zest. Women's voices, in a dream or in a drama. Timbres that compel. A shout rattles a door in its frame, sets the glass a-quiver. Three verses in a day versus failure. All lines are accounted for and none are adequate and can lead to depression if not followed. Clocks embed in every lined forehead, the pointer's edge scribes an endless circle to intersect the moment essential for rising to labour. Grope and gasp and glean. Often so adorable then wretches. The cotton thinned of stuffing, the plucked goose long ago laid down.

in moist depressions or old
campfire sites. Seems to follow humans around, move
in after they've eaten, dumped

But For Dew

Dawn pokes light, tongues the ditch edge, spots a frolicking flower, say black-eyed Susan. Nearby, closer to the woods, a rally of tint—blue flag, scarlet paintbrush, their wet gleam. A manifesto for silence and deep sight written beside the quilty grasses, shades of pale peach and avocado, restful, moist. Search for a word licked like a teardrop from velvety skin, as unexpected tenderness rises out of slumber before the thickness of the day sets in. A riot of yellow, orange, crimson bobs in a breeze of dreamy words, right here, paged and caged, or beside you in a vase, smooth-necked, as it ought to be. Gambol, gentle sway (already said). New consciousness rises and it's not fundamental. Laziness necessary to creation before the seventh day. A slipped-in description—just one fluid point of view—to do with first thought, poets and lovers and guttural sounds. Buzzy work ethic of insects that live one day or one week is a marvel often referred to with swat and squash. In the stomach a rumble makes the tongue reach for salt and honey. A stone, picked up on the sandbar as the river rushes by, held in a pale palm, is the blush of rising sun or a petal sudden in its bloom.

and **moved** on.

Red Bryum . Bryum miniatum
Noticeable for its redness—

Incumbent Lilies ... Always Softer Than

Elizabeth Willis, a flowery determination in her name, is precise, even when she breaks the rules and flashes wit. Grammatical errors have names though memorizing them does not relieve their weight. She's attracted to the droplet on a petal in the morning light. Careful study in repeated fashion reveals recurrences. The road along the canal dusted chalk-fresh with virgin snow is trackless, the gravel trucks have steered a different route. In another case a halo was invented when he missed the post office, drove right by. To speak of flowers and snow indicates a longing. And pretty too. A novice astronaut is not beyond earthly fantasies and dons peculiar disguises in the name of love—say, a white wig and diaper. Outer space may be wherever found and perhaps an air-locked suit is just another costume. Purity fixations of the godly godless. Consistent, official and responsible, do flowers have a conscience? No blues like the Muddy blues, the florid blues, dropping notes or petals in the fall. Nothing more faithful nor more soft than pollen on an anther.

its distinction. The uninitiated might
not know that **moss can be red**. They can be forgiven.
A red cushion, a

Cooking Into Glass

Obvious yet transparent material—a lens perhaps, a cocktail flute, a tiny window over the wing—descent over a blazed beach, stitched white between blue and green at Puerto Vallarta which seems unsafe these days. Ritzy gizmo in a fashion magazine that would be foreign in a barrio. A battery and a light on a tube looks like a magic wand despite its clumsiness and the need to wave and swoop. Beauty is in the eyes that have it. You are sixty-two and will never look like that unless you're Yoko Ono, even older and with sunglasses and terrific limbs. She poses in a black mini in a magazine and appears mysterious and self-conscious, a wounded heroine, caught. In the Rocky Mountains in Canada above the Bow River a flock of geese in February skies well before St. Valentine's seems early though the mail brings a heart-shaped card that sets a tune on wing. A globule, glassy, palm-sized, is oval and smooth and promises to communicate. After dark and a click the shiny screen offers erotic dance and makes you wonder how the love of god can hold one chaste. It curves like the moon, shines white with its light, the illusive halo. Silica enters the kiln and comes out with a molten gloss and is blown into defining and defying shapes. Flick the switch and more skin flips before your eyes. You'd roll in the snow if she were here—Yoko, that is. Meanwhile, the dancer on the TV screen astounds in the placement of her endless muscled legs.

red carpet, stitched to exposed
rock, brings red softness to a hardrock (not redneck) life;
brings music

The Stolen Pear

Phrase is dropped from *pop* (culture) to *pyrus* (arboreal genus), initial letters found to be the same. The fresh-from-oven-bread-waft spreads its sweet and oaty scent to nuzzle in the nose. A fruitloaf, a pillow of sensation so thick it beckons a head to drop to it. Fahrenheit or centigrade cause degrees of confusion. A framed harvest returns to haunt the tension of the lines. Done and set beside the fruitful bowl, looks like a Cézanne still-life. Snow on the deck-chair, a cushion too. No forbidding or theft at the window but with curtains filled with holes to let the light, the room a blossom. A wish to give Ms. Willis another cameo but a wish is not enough to spot her in the street, or in a hooded parka, but possibly in the evolution section of the Olin Memorial Library. Argentina Santos' fado, in iPod headphones, moves *saudade* over the ocean to a listener's ears into his body, slows him and bends him ever-so-slightly, though not a word is in his ken. Yet a hike props the whole day up and might enable a grasp of psychological truth and a sense of pick-pocketing the day. Never forget to include spirit in every piece, even if uncertain what to say. Speak a rhythm with a juicy mouthful, the soundtrack a spirited aubade. Heroes of the word lead to strangeness, love and rubato's patterned spontaneity. A challenge to break and go on; a bite, a puff into hands cupped over the lips, a glimpse through winter's early grab, a tree splendid, still bounteous with its gold and russet, its swollen seeds unseasonably released.

of red—sunset, wine and fire engine;
Flush
of red—lust, embarrassment, hypertension;

41

For Sale The Painted Gun

The field a veil of white, a palette of Malevich and Agnes Martin's delicate insistent minimalist grid. The walker pulls from a pocket two pellets—one tiny, grey, plucked from an unknown bush, the other, a rosehip, wrinkled red—to keep him safe from spirits and ghosts. Against the river's flow and between nudging ice doilies two ducks swim and bump toward the ice-free edge. A dog presses her snout to any rock or tree, any odour—a study in immodesty—but seldom runs in crow-straight lines. Give up— the way to go—surrender to it. *Surrender*, as Elvis sang it, is a word that's lost an aspect in this time of levelled guns and lives. Cheeks rosy, too, though nothing is beneath the dignity of television. Sun shone through and now the grey settles in—it's always been this way so why the fuss, the observation? A topless head, a severed hand. Nothing left to bargain in the planetary store. In the story told through dance, dancers sponge on green-tinged body-wash to translate the music of an earthly angel. In horticultural zone two, it's tough to keep skin supple without painting on the lotion. Among the circus tents, the improvised explosives, how to find the true path, even if filled with danger. Words evaporate when pursued and with Kapalbhati Pranayama and in the asana known as Adho Mukha Svanasana or Downward-facing Dog. Hands and feet pressed to earth, lips closed, throat-back brought to awareness, eyes soft focus, all engaged in a tilt against futures-trading, profit-grab—already disarmed, already in a downturn, yet, against the graven, against gravity, pushing up.

To a rock's inertness.
Pulse
of red—heart, blood, a wailing newborn

A Form Of Tuning

Over German wine and Asian noodles one confused diner speaks in tongues, the unspeakable speaking through. The unnamable soaked up in its contemplation. Weary and afraid of avalanche the teacher chooses nonetheless to hum and trudge halfway into the mountains to meet a luckless lover. A day for commitment approaches on the blown-in path. A strum or two, a twisted knob, a test—"one-two, one-two"—of harmonics. Beavers emerge in winter to gather twigs to shore up the roof; the evidence, tracks with drag aimed to a hole in the ice, to moving water. The know-the-angles fold-out died of a heavy overdose of fame. Flame crackles in the fireplace, draws stress-fled guests and a dog asleep at their feet, all bathed in heat. The observer watches for operational signs, and instead inserts a hair space. Spicy sauce clings to fingers and reminds him of a time gone by, a dinner, a forehead's articulation of sadness, a memory he'd rather flee, not savour. Perhaps after eight is too late for contemplation or composition, if going for broke or broken heart. Three men sue a baby for her fortune and DNA will testify. *Prosit!* and the udon elongates, wiggles off the chopstick. It's in the ear really, and a matter of relationship, for who has perfect pitch or a guarantee of success? Aim, strive, learn the qualities of snow, proper uncorking, how to handle the fretful and the fretboard, how to tie a Windsor a reef a love knot and never end with a question.

Bryum bears such a weight
on its spongy shoulders
in its blunt, concave, oblong leaves—to

43

As Forgiveness, Get

Sun makes the snow-mounds pink beyond the ice-doily convention in the backwash bay. Need you beg? The walker removes his fur hat suddenly wary of being thought to be an animal breaking into view of the hunter who steps slowly off his ATV. On your knees or just give in. A brown bunny so static it's mistaken for a bush or stone. The walker wishes he'd worn a yellow John Deere vest, or a bright red hat. He pays his penance, paces on nerve-crushed feet. Tiny creature tracks to the edge of the ice. How far to go to escape the rumble of trucks. How far to go to do no harm. Look away and the blush is gone. The rabbit too, like the lover who once graced his hands, now invisible. With a roar the quad spurts over the hill. Gravel spits. A sigh in the world, or is it a gasp.

represent **otherness**, the reddest
of reds, to show all mosses **what's**
beyond being green.

Everything Heavy Falls

The road leans beside skeleton trees toward their whiteness, then ends. A sad song has weight that bends the listener to contemplate pain and mortality, from city to countryside. Sunglasses shoved carelessly into the backpack scrape the book's cover, carve a scar, etched and forever, upon the container for words' delicacies, allure and porosity. Then steps, winding, you might say, among the trees, a hoof-trodden narrow path, a signature, a melody of animal breath. Sits like ammo, awaits the snap of the cocked hammer in the traveller's heart. A joke or a tale—the one about the elephant in the room or the whacko with a gun. "Let's have a conversation and get it out," that thin membrane that holds the truth too screened and vulnerable to allow the silences that fill with need. Fire or chocolate on the tongue. The heart blooms with inadequacies. The gifted poet of song whose voice sings with tenderness and ache from his too soon final years. Hinge-squeal of the gate thrown open to let the traveller back from solitude to society. No separation between the trail and the grass, grass and heaven. John Lennon sits the next seat over. You don't have to believe this despite its truth, or, whether speaking metaphorically, to hit gas or brake, to acquiesce and forgive, or to take up arms. Yet the light, once dancing weightless, crumbles.

Hairy Screw Moss . Tortula ruralis
Those taxonomists—what
a sense of humour. The libido

Read Her For Bursts

Any word replaceable. The motel is called The Alpine though far from the Alps and run by a Korean family, polite and happy in their enterprise. Fat white benedictions of snowflake. Can't stop fingered motion over keys or words—it's everywhere, in living rooms, in taxis, in shopping malls—a thumb and lip taxonomy. Qi Gong gestures and beliefs for healing—rotating knees and persecution. Salmon with dill and a sharp white Italian wine. Eyes scan to correct the typography, followed by the movement of deft hands and words unthought of. Early larks explode from the skeletal bush beside the river and make the heart skip as if a winner at an award ceremony. Are they waxwings, warblers, or tea leaves read in the bottom of a cup? A journey in the future will involve quantities of chai that will keep the sipper up late at night, skipping to the loo (my darlin') and worried like a dog at a bone, gnawing on splintered conflicts, listening in stereo to Ani DiFranco talk down the bushwhacked regime, its cruelty and lies, and possibly a tall dark stranger, all while driving. Snow mounts on the teak deck table, teak a long way from its forest of origin and heat. See whatever skirmishes into the open but be unable to read its signs—you'll be average. A dog is loyal, a blotter for attention. The traveller skims her books as bread goes sour, erupts with mould-buds, on the crust, on the cusp of forget.

of moss, any way you like it. Libertine.
Dark green or reddish brown—
But wait, it's unisexual

Could Word Belie Its Little

Hail the ones who are tender lovers more than once and escape tragedy, almost. Tomorrow's redemption with word and song. In the café in the neighbourhood with character and trend-caché, two dishy women with gym-trim sportswear curves twist in their seats and gab with intensity. The cell phone rings, a call from the place where animal tracks lead to a tiny hole in snow beside the grass clump, and the words seem smaller, distant. A glass teapot bought for dharma, the drama of the spectacle of plumping flowery leaves. Some people can't comprehend metaphor in the name of the law. About cooking chicken. The east has come to the west that wants its wisdom right away. What matters about that? Gunpowder tea might blow the lips off conversation. A menu and a book by the same name is all that is needed en route to the gates, the set table, as the observer imagines these two beauties in his kitchen in aprons, dressing the bird. No need for small talk, once sparkly aperitifs have been served, to open the buds or betrayal. Such tiny footprints along the wall and just a slight waver from the straight and true. Daffodils spring from a fluted crystal vase. Serve a lover with or without a name and forget your own, but be in love as dawn whispers over the sill, over unclad thighs.

and spreads itself around
from sea to alpine slopes
in crevices and on the skin

Crouching In The Umber

He walks every day the same path by the stream, up the hill, across the plain, then bends to enter the woods and finds all time collapsed as one continuous walk in the familiar and his memory walks with him in what might be a moment of enlightenment if only he could be sure. Rabbit, almost missed, sits on the dark soil under a bush all fuzz and branch, a twitchy whisper as the eye zooms in. To cope with clutter try to sort and pack some off, though there's always a catch. Hops in and out of view between grass and boughs, light and shade. Moving words around satisfies though does not guarantee improvement but might be a lever yet it's possible that fewer are better. A rusty tractor-bucket full of firewood motors through the charcoal-etched treelines. Use paragraphs or couplets of clattery hardware to find inherent resonance. Gasoline grabbed by mistake instead of diesel compromises a motor and a word. All manifestoes, no matter how stark, have an element of truth. The girth of a chef and his laboured puff as he bends to a shelf to retrieve a pot is no measure of his skill, or a politician's appetite. Observe the determination of cedars, chopped and lopped (intimidation—foreign, relentless) as they send new branches out and upward with fervour every spring. Why not an oval nozzle? They predict low profits for natural gas, with reserves overfull and hair-tearing accountants and CEOs, leading to male pattern baldness. Let's not burn more books, which creates smoke and blindness. Next day he'll walk and stoop again through the brown shadows of the alder copse, stepping in his own footprints that lead the way.

of rocks, curves
back when wet and twists
upright

Itching Satellites

Space is scratched with probes. Fingers tickle the circle of navel above the low-rise waistband. You don't necessarily want to eat a cookie in the computer age or send static from the toxic carpet to your pussycat or keyboard or walk too close to cooling towers that emit rays you can't feel in your skin, today. A megalomaniac rises from nowhere every quarter century, but melanoma is much more frequent. The appearance of women, their fashion choices and forms of representation, bump through many years and in the male poem, and must be on their own terms to make gains in the social sphere, now being reclaimed, even in the veiled world. Out there circling all the time. Even in a line, a measure of the length of the penis. Don't be fooled by branding. All those channels surge through air that seems empty, but so breezy, yet collision is inevitable, so the growing risk of hazardous debris. The game is on ice, with fat pretzels and beer, where salary caps outshine transcendent quest. Monks sing, don't sin, they shine, but thin. A lozenge or a lemon every day for constant health. Space is not big enough but will go on red-shifting longer than we know or can imagine. Sleep would love to keep you, and it will. What can a tart wear nowadays besides a fluted collar?

when dry. Earthy, wild,
ungroomed—the baser instinct of the shod and trodding ones.

Fan Moss . Rhizomnium **glab**rescens

49

All Of You To Spend

Preoccupied with nose hairs when the economy goes out of control. Ducks skim and dive and rise from the river oblivious to spring's delay or the likelihood of manifestoes cashing in. A rhyme's a poem's zest, the gnarled syntagmatic root its brace. Time for tea and pleasantry. Some people are water organisms, sponge and leech. The sun a veiled glow through a linen apron that flaps on the line. Leafless grey poplar boughs are tufted. The disappearing arts of spinning wool and yarding ale. At the end of a line of credit we kite ourselves away. If we could control our own release of pheromones and lure desired ones at will then life would be philharmonic. The superstore is a deranged sensorium that wants to eat each surplus in a purse. By the window, a flicker of chickadee whose tiny brain recalls her elaborate cache-map, but hides more than she reclaims. Nature is always there, wanting in. Welcome sun that breaks the clouds, endangers by its dazzle. The waist the apron will clutch and articulate with a bias and a knot, deficit and a bond.

Immodest, with naked
stems and unisexual (which does not mean indiscernible, but
singular—like people, well

As If I'm Looking

Stolen, sweet, that moment with the beloved son, on the telephone between this and that obligation, son's visage in the father's third eye. Popcorn and pop-goes-the-weasel are moments to remember as long as you can live. Peer through time's gate and pretend it's all there despite the lock. Laundry tomorrow and the last supper. Rabbit trails distinct, plentiful in the snow. Car thieves drove through the night, with their load of contraband booze, right through the gate, in sight of the camera and panicked at video surveillance, skidded to a halt, turned around, to escape a plot that unfolded, re-folded in the dry clank and static crease of walls and bars, and yes, surveillance. Society reports could not be more weird than they are today—tales of addictions and adoptions, gowns and guns. A peculiar blip of sunspots. Get eyes moving with the times to read the uncharted articulations of Spinoza. Wind blew and burned his face and it hurts several hours later, so he'd take a kiss there. Or sip more wine, German, fresh and slightly sweet. Too much fermented grape soaks into pages, though the host charms, accommodates, is gracious with her wares and taste, a bright and luscious invitation to the eye. "It's a book that needs some spine," quipped the critic. The extraordinary resonance of everything appears before a stilled eye at the moment it closes to the dark.

most of them).
Males a bit foppish with rose-like clusters of leaves at the tip
and the gals with their usual capsule, their receiving cup.

Drive Without Drowning

Eight goals and he's a super-star. How proud he was and Ezra Pound waits on tape beside the player. It was fun and he got a Hawaiian shirt in the deal. The house packed with dreams of Hollywood. Generosity sets off a chain of events like the cliché of butterflies in China and something unexpected happens with the format and navigating the canal road with success. Directions on the mirror seem askew and pointed stumps mark evidence of beavers-chew. Spelling is irrelevant when chanting begins or when Tina Turner struts her age-defying gams and bewitchery. Pop culture enters our dreams and will we rise or sink? There's a suit and even a five-month-old needs a lawyer to stay afloat. Cheese and pesto on the crusts makes a nice accompaniment, unexpectedly, to a biryani dinner. He opted for packages, though was reluctant to wear tights. Every day a new poet is discovered by a different reader who meets a resonant sensibility, though strange. Hauling wood stirs thought from chunks to trunks to the splendour of trees, yet a fireplace comforts and warms many spent hands. The word *chainsaw* rips ahead and evokes fear where blood's a possibility and fearlessness evokes a summit of achievement, an undercurrent, or an underbite that binds and lashes back.

When wet they spread wide, and when dry shrivel
to the stem, like a penis after ejaculation, like a clitoris becalmed
but they prefer the decadent, the low elevations, hanging

Against Azure, Coherent

The facts do not come from the words *flood* or *television*, though both suggest blue, but from the deep churn that turns all brown. How to keep your hands free of the blade, nose pointed north, wheels on the road across the black ice. After his faux pas, he was unaware, even though there were snickers. Deer tracks cross coyote tracks in angular directions— coincidence, cross-purposes, deadly courtship? You'd think ideas would stop coming after dark. *Chocolate bar* across the osmotic waters of stark hunger. A rise in tone when advice is given, and often careful structure. Everything scrubbed clean before the linguist could lend a hand to each sentence that seemed too short and had the same rhythm, but held together, if not monotonous. The pool-playing brother has taken his last shot across the green felt, the eight-ball preceding him to the dark pocket. A debt to pay with coins, a wash, still damp, to lay out. Who is speaking? One more day, then it's back to reality, but shut it off now for comfort, in mind at least, as everything falls, or falls together. This obsession with empty celebrity. You'd rather sit on a trunk by white sheets flapping on a pole beside bright pueblos, nestled, exotic, above lapping indigo, where you hope to glimpse your intention. Who are you, and *you*?

out on rotten logs and in humus (not hummus), a
common sort, and bearing contradictions.

Lover's Moss . Aulacomnium androgynum

Erased Porridge

A gruelling trail, a trial of gruel. Appeals and appalls. He was sessile, shy, though not beyond the sway of swasivious invitations. Body rituals turn us into ritual bodies. Your grandma knew it'd stick to your ribs, provide oomph all day. You'd eat it but she is forever gone. The dictionary and the missing word. He hadn't read the essential passage of Gary Snyder's walking mountains and so missed the gist. A new cloak of hoarfrost on the branches makes small organic Popsicles, brings a taste of beauty to a curious tongue even though the licker has to squint into the radiant fire of sun on chilly Saint Valentine's Day. The latent Eros of Thai massage or hands tied to a bedpost with lacy rose-coloured lingerie. We live in Orwellian times, though George does no longer, but saw them coming even though his name was Eric. Dip fingers into concavity and bowl on. Stick a spoon to your face and face a crowd of non-believers. It's all ridicule and radical and possibly physics. Shooting for bondage or science or love, who can roll the dice in overtime en route to Heaven, and be sure of an oaty win?

Goes **either** way, or no way, being andro.
But appropriately reddish at the tip, like all **lovers**.
A small and modest plant, **vulnerable** and

On My Wastedness

Who has clean hands? Place them there on a scab with an "Oh!" At loose ends hollow hopes are strung along by a thin one with orbital hips. The military precision of the fashion runway but with more sashay—raw, raucous and rattling—a styled dare. Sun brings frost's message to a tolerable level and diminishes its rococo scrolls on the pane. Truth hidden beyond the next glance or horizon stays hidden. Books in boxes still speak despite the stack and closed lids. Departure is soon, though the stone sits on the stump, urges stillness. Lovers out there, waiting, wanting, waning. Intolerant dark, and a flashing light beacons its way through the curtain of snow. Haul in the firewood, haul in the gourmet meal and try to forget agonies, a clog of ashes in the hearth. Read and be read, then someone, please spin a clue from the spokes that hold the rim embraced by the flayed rubber, once a cushion. Slip on a snazzy suit to hide shreds of shady character and hope to flip the odds. Glamorous lips pucker in the glossy desert pages. Or slip on a disaster suit and slide into the adjacent photograph of the nuclear test site.

all cushion and tuft. And when love
goes dry, the moss withers and presses
its tufts into its thin stalk. But when flourishing

Clouds Reflected In The Gutter

Bricks, sludge, and the fly-by bomber jets all shine in the dark oil gleam. Words always wait to cluster, cumulus and serious, even in rubble. The seeker walks a spiritual path without knowing what's underfoot. Often heard to say "Peaches and tranquility, some just deserts." Today the world whirs and precipitation crashes the soil and disastrous wind topples ancient trees. Tresses flow molten on the pixel screen. Once a poet said "the poem is a bowl with slippery sides"—words as corn-flakes, a few crumbs stuck in the bottom after the meal. It's a count-and-spend life, to alter a phrase. A fungus on-the-loose in paradise and we're armed with blanks. Lipstick is blood, the nightstick is blood, the lollystick is blood. Skin cream ads adorn the Superbowl. A meditation where little is revealed in the repeated walk through words, the wooded path, hikers scraping thin topsoil down to rock, right down to finest sand, a sluice-fault bed. Bob and twitch, the busy-ness of the tiny bird at the feeder etching survival in the winter sun. On every route, slime clings, soils all the boots. The seeker, occupied with muck, once looked up, and through scrimmed vapours, new beauty glimpsed.

prefers thrill and **novelty**, can
bring **life** even to the **burnt** and blackened.
With the **heat** of desire and regeneration

Dropped My Glove To Find You

Scuffle in the low brush. Water in the high-lipped bucket keeps the snakes from slithering out. Braces hurt the youngster's mouth and cut his tongue. Grim today but never grim enough. Knocked and dripped in the thaw, the sliding closet door sets off a rumble. In the early days gangs held forth and threatened, one led by a tough named Curly who proved that true sons-a-bitches overcompensate for lack, in terms of verticality. Ping-pong-pinball mind, a schemed belief that snakeskin makes a dandy though the casually cast-down item's not a new ruse, but a disguised, yet obvious coaxing an osculum. No such thing as accident. Glances spell and expel an ostrich plume of random thought in courting display. She bends at the waist and there is much to see, enough to ache her back, his loin, on rising. The hell that wells when help's not found sobs on the telephone, a hammer ping in the ear. There's a centrifuge somewhere that'll bear her weight and whirl it free. Whee! "Gee, love'll find you," says the myopic oculist, "pick it up," he continues, tests for slipperiness or solid ground. "All done," she says, waving the castaway toward the dandy, with a smile that beckons. On the nearby grim-field, shrapnel shards find and eat up skin.

soothes the cut and scarred.

False Polytrichum . Timmia austriaca
How does a moss know?

Our Startled Shade

The pursued sues the suitor. A shotgun marriage awaits the frisky tailor in the shadows of fine stitchery. A tanned manager concerned with the softening midriff hid inside his dark tailored suit would go back to the gym if the snow was not so paralyzingly white. Exhalation learns to plow a lock through a human throat. Or if you prefer, coppice. Language is a rabbit-hat-trick-landscape where chill wind rattles through the first and second chamber of discontent. Cows lazed, laced single-file across the ridge appear to be a slow freight that chugs toward the escape horizon. A question of geometry. The virus in his air passage is almost gone, but where? Neck as a straw. Ducks float beneath the sun though the rays do not penetrate surprise. A great day for spirals around a clump of needle-grass, with no hint of aliens. As if not strange enough, the *ostranenie*, not stretched or strenuous. There go the boxcars now, sucked by the whistle's vacuum through an iris. Read the syllable as a bullet.

A **trickster** and a mathematical **genius**,
not the real *polytrichum*, but the
tricky one—it's in the name. And those translucent

Moss If It Gathers

A green parrot is called Random on a card. A son, the only one, laughs whacky as a lace curtain flaps against the marble table in the turbulent wind at angles changing and incalculable. Artisan cheese is a labour of love and the purity of milkers. Shakespeare's tale of love inspired Tchaikovsky's *Fantasy Overture* which seeks the essence of the tragedy and may speak to you. On the white napkin, stones stack their crenulations, striations and modesty, as small feathery green sprigs crumble off. Romeo is the name of a coffee-brewing machine which has a tiny balcony. To begin the accumulation of intensities, violins enter at just the right moment. A phone call with despair and tears at the end of the line launches a challenge over lunch. The fifty-second state is the state of depression. The sixty-second workout is a lie. Clustered there and waiting for rain, sex forms an umbrella in wetter recollection. A line from elsewhere echoes in the head, clogs all the channels of poetry and possibility where cedar rot may not cushion a fall. On the grey rocks on the bank by the river on a summer day, the woman screams as a snake crosses her path, screams not "love," but her spouse's name, not a phenomenon at thirty below, the snake, that is. Plumbers and playwrights and political advisors sweat and swear, but are not social workers equipped with safety gear, or personal trainers, or agronomists. We anticipate and long for, to cushion us, the season of aulacomnium androgynum.

cells—now you see 'em, now you don't—
the leaf cells are square, not odd-shaped or simply
irregular, but square, so back to the math thing—and those

59

A Smudge Against

Eye relative to irritant specks of dust. A painting is viewed elaborately. Tears and swirling pigeons. A hazardous windshield, pocked and cracked. Blonde tresses bounce. From protein backwards, welding joy with obsession and a dark rub along the branded monogram of alligator. On the side of a truck, a muffin the size of a blown-up cow patty slips past dazzling red high heels and a curve of calf, sidewalking. Speak, Elizabeth—is that you with a Tom Waits rasp? Mote motet. Motors rev up the hounding drought. Viscerebral. Infiltration flux, anticipated, erases, replaces. A brush with colour bristles just so. All teeth and Burberry scarf geometry, leaned into. On a balcony of exclusive condos in the upscale shopping zone, an orange pylon. Clown hat or hazard cone, it blemishes, chuckles, it points and signs, awaits arrival or a swerve.

peristomes on the sporophytes—the inner with 64 **filaments**, the outer with 16 teeth—64 being four times 16—what's that about? —**remember** the square leaf cells? 4 squared, and 4 to the third **power!**

Lodged Or Branches

"Tighter and lower." The fit these days. But the city reaches for a sky-full of static electricity. A dram of cask-strength single malt to lift or lean him beyond the house that needs repairs, beyond a heart abused. The tile-board sodden, spongy. Jeans whose waistband tortures hips and keeps crotch and ass awareness constant. Live-in appendages seem bandaged and appear to reach toward the bondage/dominance fulcrum, a strange anti-arboreal splendour, as-but-though against nature. A golden curry subtle and scrumptious. An attitude of sharing and enthusiasm over a piece of sonic art while remembering that pair of plush cheeks nudged against the bar in a seedy but gentrified part of town, a secret tucked away, a seam on display. Walking through an etude of memories of twenty or fifty years ago, today, the lanes seem smaller, the houses narrower, the past a diminuendo. Coffee bar closed for the night serves disappointment. A twinge in the heart, a pain or hard-to-shake longing on the subway stairs. What kind of trouble can be found that bares a saving grace? Failed hope, dark sticks that scratch inside the skull. The streetcar jolts on uneven track, sends the returned visitor, now a tourist, a-sprawl in the aisle, the clutch-strap dangling overhead.

That moss knows **something** it's not telling.

Goblin's **Gold**. *Schistostega **pennata***
You think you've got it tough! This one is a wonder.

Nearly Touching The Eye Of A Horse

Softens the air with its tender stare, almost sad. And a flutter. Is that the
word an equestrian would use? High-school girls in a flock twitter at the
gate, focusing the light. Pools at the lid-bottom. Scent of a stable rises
to his nostrils slightly flared. A neighbourhood where neighbours are
strangers, hooded in their concerns. He talks and talks about a crumbled
basement, a house in shambles, a love still held despite packed boxes and
moving trucks. Pain is constant, trots an oval, always back. Her boots are
thick, her legs thin sticks. A dream of a royal neighbourhood, a neigh that
takes the mind out of town's sad abandonment. The weed man pauses
with his wound hose and tubs of herbicides. What's the point of asking
for forgiveness, the grass unpalatable? Hoof-ground, hoop-shot. An arc,
a chunk in thought, a gaze not understood, though soft with trust before
a hovering hand.

Can live in a cave or under up-turned tree roots
and in depressions with little light. But they're diminutive. These little guys
produce filaments that have lens-shaped cells to concentrate light—

62

Fiction To The Boot

Encased. Sit in a plush chair and stare at the glassed-in waterfall, the shimmering mortared rock wall, a sun-struck glint. Truth's toe-punt into the empty net, or faux snakeskin from the pointy toe-tip, high over the calf and shapely. Stories as made or what's made of them. Scientists whisper "doom" and governments answer "cluster-bomb." A mood of quietude and dislocation rustles through the masses, a discomfiting silk. Silt settles on a small ear-piece beside selfish lips. Soldiers, heavy-footed, break step on the bridge to prevent sympathetic vibrations, crescendo and collapse. Cholesterol may be a tale of high-living. He calls himself Electric Bill and writhes, charged as he performs, while Sasha sells cashews in the posh hotel lobby above the underground passages of mercantile fetish. A night so late and so latted. Good shoes and lots of black. Ride the rails through resistant spring and a constant whistle. Wormholes crawl through dense mass at the centre of the story's black hole, black soul, a black sole trodding on the plot that waits, lost sight of in the shiny grass. Through prismed droplets and scissored rails, words at once offer promise and fissure.

what light there is—enables them to grow. They form
golden, gleaming mats of thread—
like plants. Just

Who Elevates The Evening

A folded page, folded legs, a fold of skin near darkness. Bar stool, piano stool, café stool. Ups and downs on youth-filled streets. Sore feet lead to sit, then act up, swell up, and a brush with foreign tongues that wobble off the straining ear. He waved the empty bottle for a refill in the late night *charamba* jubilation, ill-mannered perhaps. *La même chose, merci. Le chardonnay.* Up the high steps with iron railings, slush everywhere. *There's always one or two more in April just when you think it's over.* Shift poems away from symptom and prediction. Friday night and the town waits beyond the automatic doors. The royal mount incurs a drive around to hear George Bowering lift baseball poems from the page and laughter from the lips of the assembled. So long to get there through the streets that parade with confidence and style. Blend savoury spice and daring fashion and see old friends through serendipity and intention. Time of long and slow. How many cars will it take to run the universe off the road? Applause and a bow and the wine appears. Time takes itself, as everyone gasps, and eyes jerk to her lemon yellow shoes clacking on the grey slate steps.

watch for the golden sheen.

*Menzies' Neckera . **Met**aneckera **men**ziesii*
Perhaps the diamond-shaped

A Letter, A Pagan

A cluster of words betrays absence, sealed with a tongue. The diary is incomplete. Pain so old he marvels at its intensity today, day worn sharp and edgy with a sense of repetition. Wild abandon, body paint, unsanctified spirit worship, nakedness, leads to other knowing, to a fall, the moral walls danced through. A new duality, double-edged blade that slits, slips along the seal to open a wealth of news or puff of foreign air. Score and snore are attitudes to the puck chase. Gestures across a counter's fit of exchange. The currency of stamps, the stomp or stammer of a speaker upon the studied air. An air of clarification. New flowers poke from her nervous hands, from thawing soil's discomfort. An order to things well beyond twenty-six to the *nth* power. Apparently immoral ones thrust their wanton bodies. Who's to judge, to say what's decadent? A soldier's cap, a skirt extra-short, a German auto that bestows prestige. Correspondent words prance, unpreened, yet turn out and scent the aisle with ardour, the odour of the future.

smooth leaves, **desirable** to
brides-in-waiting, **brides**, drawn
to its **leaves**, strongly transversely.

Understanding Rock Time

Rays of light reach through the wormholes. Every stone a collapsed universe. He was called seer, prophet, lunatic, and still hovers. Heaven's a machine that spins belief from threads of thought. Awe or fear? Terror rages, rails on the shoulders of the othered skin in sunglasses. They cage a small sporty car, red, and for profit. The motive keeps us moving. The coffee customer's hat is brown corduroy, doffed and clutched to a tight bundle in his left hand. Bobbing spirits shift among first spring-sprouts of lilies, poke between garden-stones, bearing knowledge. Skirts emerge seasoned in a shorter form. Form is what takes the eye, draws desire with a pulsing urgency. Beware the gerund, the pebble in the air, the swaying branch, the sandstone you dance on, it slips or bullets. He is synonymous with illumination and visions—that poet—his words though, slate-dark now, to most eyes, but not to those who see beyond. What's known clicks over, an amnesic clock, a subdued ache, a tumbled safe-lock click—click, click, click … a rock that ricochets, ticks, talks.

wavy. An **olive**-green mat-mantle
descending from the **shoulders of** coniferous
trees, found wherever coastal **brides**

To Hide The Virtues

Wrote *coincidence* for *conscience*, obviously a dislocated mind. He abandons the given, riven and riveted, and hammers on. Splinters, slivers here, spiked in skin, in a frame of words weighted with sight and moral sense at the edge. Mortal senses—*la nature morte*—still or lively? Chance may play but there's a reason for a good act. Feint or fate guided by a past life. Coins as cons or icons. If the brain is chemistry what is spirit? Breath wants more of itself but fights the tight chest, the worried jaw. The hunter, lying low, beads us in his scope, our vulnerable skulls, hats pulled down. It is time to stand and fear no cleanliness, uncover what is pure. No matter whether white or wrinkled and rimmed in a shadow's grip. The stark trees loosen their hold on plumping buds. A song that mourns moves toward exaltation. Hearing strains, suffers the ringing of our suppositions.

are at low-lying elevations (that is **hardly**
elevation at all) and on cliff
faces, calcium-rich, bone place, bone-**bound**, offering

A Breeze To Sweet-Talk

Aubade comes first as dedication. Spring, and dust is everywhere, and tears. Want, yes, want blows up with this and every season. She wants to cut her coffee-shots. To think she's free of clutter—a stack of paper here, unopened envelopes at the elbow and books half-read, tower toward mind's thin air intake or the tile-board ceiling; words grip and glow, in their illusion. Blows through—a restless and ungraspable idea. Bob Dylan sings about her sugar and wants it, and don't we all, snorting Splenda or Sweet'N Low? A hymn for dawn, a hum to prep for trials of the too-soon day-pressed mind. The instructor calls for Exalted Warrior asana, for letting go. A cramp in the arch discomfits the yogin's foot, hampers exaltation. Candle flame with pale aura prepares (almost) for sun. Across the way, bodies halo, betray conditions unknown, even to themselves. Grit blows into eyes from the all-night-driving tractor-trailer whose eighteen wheels blast us to the curb. Why will things continue as they are? No use pretending that nothing burns, while smoke, not song, stings away the honey in the throat.

small and narrow branchlets
for the glinty gem.

Hanging Moss . Antitrichia curtipendula

68

See) A Girl Who Talks To Birds

Her hands flutter in air, a silent language made visible. A wing, sympatico, young and by the hemlock grove. Whistle and pish. Or matronly, a figurehead of fields who murmurs to low-flying grass dwellers. Her lips move too, feather the air for particles, molecules, anything to stir a sense of . . . could it be *existence*, a term, perhaps, too mundane for wonder. A creak of branches, a quaver of warbles. A heavenly tectonic shift, a quake. What falls to the ear does not always fall, nor is heard. Morning and the sun brazenly hot. This definite location does not yield its topographical coordinates. The room fills with generosity, a glug of uttered glyphs, as strangers speak. File back and forth across time's dividing, divining line. Some lost on the threshold where the light-blaze trips, a life-spent last stumble, before it hits the floor. But that was *then*, the speaker glad to say *this*, still *now*. A body makes its own dance, and fingers flit for many reasons. Sweet whispers, whooshes and tweets, an earful, air full, her lips form syllables, a heart in gratitude reaches, far as an eye flies.

Now here's **a bold** one,
makes a colour-**statement, rusty**
and **orange**, a bit brash, a bit

Glassy Horizon. My Pen

Written on a face in ink, red, a bumpy tattoo of rash and blemish that wishes a hood at its edges pulled by small self-conscious hands, the nib finer than expected, but busy. *Jests* fill the room several times, party balloons, notes sent, with or without smiles from keyboards. More nervous, self-conscious hands tilt toward walls and ceilings, anxious relative faces, and out through pores in windows in exchange for beads of evening sun. The word *Turneresque* is unexpected, unusual with its three *E*s, two *U*s, two *R*s and hangers-on *T, N, S, Q* (reminds of Ionesco), and the rescue of Turner or should we say *honouring*, and his influence. He was always painting horizons and startling light. Ship or shift brushed across the wavy way. "Pores in windows," reminds that glass is fluid fixed and breathes like skin, more solid though than proximate air. George Oppen, peers through, wants to come in, *Tho the face, still within it*. Come ahead, through the door, between glasses. Time's lock slips. *Place over which time passes*. A slip of air buffs the chest, flutters there, a connect/disconnect, a sail's flap, a flinch of awe and terror. Oppen speaks across the porous divide of being and gone and following, right here right now, as if a-sail on Turner's radiant light. George says *a false light*, not meaning the nervous movement of the brush, but the illusion of time as blemish erased. There's the glass, clear, over there, past the black and white keys, the scratched-over page, the luminous canvas. A note descends toward his craft, sails on spare open waters.

of a carrot-top and
ballooning at that and matted with Afro and Rasta hair
and making common moss uneasy

Contention Like The Damp

In fleet windows trees pass, though enter here, swirled and bound in wind's havoc. No time for concentration to bog down efficiency. Pull through bent notes toward the other side of understanding, bowed notes heard, as if a first time, a new bloom. Scent of polished wood and the sharp but earthy waft of resin. Note that softens concrete walls, makes them permeable, as if lacking substance, though the bench is hard, hips shift on it, wait, and hope for comfort. A name is called *privilege*; a young boy shuffles forth in a starched white shirt, hands clutch the instrument that often disagrees with him, clutching music's ancient dream. A small storm brews, a flutter in his chest, sweat breaks on his brow. Threat and promise. Everything poised on finger's arch and fret. Here notes will sing, while others of note far away are plucked and felled. The line of bodies and severed ears is long. A dry mouth, its tongue rolls against the teeth. Parchment skin. As if the day scraped to make itself known. Here, music transcends the strings; there, wrists burn, are unable to fly free of the rope.

with such a display. A festoon—yes it said that—
festooning tree trunks and branches
in gaps where light can break

A Negative Dreamboat

Sooner or later it turns up—a phrase or a dip in the momentum. One day smooth sailing, the next everything jumps to reverse and contrasts. The windshield spotted with rain and synchronized with wipers. Water plunges to water all around. The boat tilts, an angle that jars. An appointment, calendar-enforced, must be kept for the sake of reputation, opinions and sleek data. A plush chair will hold the talker who seeks to keel beyond blame, the margin of error. Across the grey tabletop, a cooling cup of tea slides, stops just before the edge, tips the slightest liquid onto its saucer's lip. A fair boy scowls from battle scenes to drumsticks and beats a rhythm clear and loud but with the faintest hesitation. Another song floats through fifty inky years and notes the beauty of the human voice in harmony, the thrill of falsetto sailing over the bass-deep deep. All from the stage and later from the groove in the vinyl spin. The world's a too imperfect place for ego, though you'd never know by news. Someone's rocking. It's a contradictory, counter-intuitive tack, but the prow turns toward suffering. The craft may lighten and rise if a perfect pitch sounds beyond the slip.

in at low elevations. Why
climb when you
can shock right here by just hanging

Lifts And Shoots

Demand the excoriation of rust. The greening season pushes through the thawing soil or pulses on a branch in lust for light. A certain demographic thinks of spring as female and gun barrels. Reasons for lipstick and powder burn. It is difficult to re-enter after a layoff. Myths and tales hover just below the everyday—the dancer-spirit for instance who jettés from the stage, or a face peeling off with a mask. Or camouflage. A lesson for governments. A squeak in the floor overhead that jerks the chin to an angle to better orient the ear. With the dance, a steady beat of the skin of thirteen drums, the rhythm of animal hide, sticks of bone. Blisters on the hands. Time for salve and recreation. Time to flake away the crust that stiffens the joint, even if surgery's required. Prayer, exhortation, a trip to the gym, balm from the greenest bud. Whatever it takes to tone or atone, to take beauty's hand, or to hoist and aim.

around with that orange gleam.

Clear Moss: **Hooker***ia lucens*
You might assume a moral

Eyes Are Starlight

An image over-charged in nightly notoriety. What darkness promises. A glint that begs articulation. Beyond refracted circumstance there's a peering down at us, motile and reflected back. A poster flaps against a pole as cars scoot and the globe turns. A passing sway-hipped blonde and a rasping branch hooked to a fender. Her shoes have heels of luminescent rainbow glimpsed in sweeping of headlights at the curve in the road or dangling from a café stool beneath appealing ankles. They're promises, those collapsing or reflecting bodies, and he closes his eyes and still can see them. She takes his hand and places it low. Wordless and at loss. Feet on pavement an assurance of solidity in the faceless, the face-soft dark, but elevated now and airborne. Hand pushed forward into desire's gleam. Heaven looks lonely, angels fleet of wing, elusive, and ancestors reduced to specks in memory. Ask van Gogh—it's a painting and a revolution, and may be God-sent. Twinkling spurs the bristle-strokes—a butterfly wing, beam-struck, flashes blue and settles in a tree-trunk crevice for the night.

loosening, a trade, with a name
like *Hookeria*. Or **poverty's** propulsion.
Compulsion. Though flattened, it's **a ro**bust plant

... And Is Trampled

From way back, *a thousand miles* in time, a song buffs the ears with memory of darkened gyms and dancing close. Red hair at your cheek, her hand on your warm nape, yours in the small of her back. Hope is stiff, as a fluid staff of notes lifts from a gifted throat. It is alright to be lost in the *thrill* of such crush-delirium though you resist. Could say this nib at the paper is a kiss. Tenderness seems a victim underfoot, a burning wish back then, clumsy today. Blues come everyday for BB King. He's a peer of the Teddy Bears, but he still takes the stage despite their plush sound. The pen-whisperer fears he may be running out of gas, metaphorically speaking, though there's jump at the pump his ink's in a kink. Time slips away, though for some it is smashed. Which life has brought you here, feet bumping and sliding across the floor to the soft beat, the rustle of your fabrics, your broken note? *To know, know* a dance of love from head to toe from chest to chest and in between. And in some lucky hearts it truly dwells. The Bears and BB sing it now in moody light. Something sharp is caught beneath your shoe.

despite appearing limp.
Not a flasher or a strutter, but
a shy creeper, and dark at that

Riddled By Replicas

Waiting on tea, the real tea from Bengal, to warm. But you can't protect yourself from outside, despite the aroma. But carcinoma lurks, or is it California's lurch? But the tea is savoury. But a saving or amazing grace eludes. But you're caught in a spot-check. But it's a puzzle with a masquerading answer. But someone has offered an opportunity that might or might not come to fruition, but you're in and hoping and cupping the vessel to warm your hands. But the notebook is filling up. But *up* is not the right word for a book—should be *over* or *within*, but you could say it's the words replicating, but words have no will or was Burroughs right? But the tea is savoury and satisfying to a degree despite unrest. But they are bombing in Baghdad. But they are bagging in the Superstore, where love is in Muzak. But you have to record what goes. But you don't know what it is and are inept with the device.

even though **Sinatra's** sure you're nobody 'til
somebody loves you.
Mostly **in the** undesirable wet **lowlands**, where

76

They Appear, Flying

Across the night sky, white dwarfs, stars in the last stage of evolution, are thought to be ninety-seven per cent of all stars in our galaxy. Fingers rub a sweaty bristle of hair at the back of the blissed skull looking up. Blessèd are persistent thoughts and dreamy lovers. They float pilotless, drift into mind, a breeze-borne veil or virus wedging distraction, un-balancing the yogin in tree pose. In a weekend of pain anything else will do. The liver assaulted by anti-inflammatories. A sip of chamomile may comfort. Beside a window a young man, tousle-haired, eighteen or so, draws on a pad, focused like a five-year old with crayons, and nearby a blonde-hair-with-flip girl and new-style-horn-rimmed boy, tentative on first date, an aura swirling through and over them, a delicious aching charge. Life's a putt, a pit bull, a pet peeve, biting or loving, or asleep snoring. Bound to feel it, then go for a walk with the dog and someone makes a joke and the air is relieved of tension. It's sherpa-scale, carrying the life-load that at first looks small and feather-light but weighs on the up-slope, and some can't anymore. "Too obscure," they say. Hockey laps on baseball, baseball on basketball, basketball on tennis and always the world game and all about money circling the globe, a stratosphere that promotes and pollutes with its doppelganged solitary-communal passions. Greedies, Goodies, Kamikazes, Jihadists, Buyers, Bomb-belt-wearers, Drunks, Needle-sharers, Holy-kneelers, Celebrity-stalkers, Celery-chewers, Lured and Lurers, the black hole they can't soar past. Come back everyone! Come back, all you stars! Palm our cheeks, nuzzle our necks, glide light to the corners of our mouths, cup us in the span of your gleam.

it lives on **moist** humus, where the poet
misread most **humans**, while checking his skin for clear moss **clusters**
and finding none, and acknowledging his privilege

Her Body In The Dark

Imagined or accompanied. Needless to say, there's awareness of flesh and blindness involved. The brush of other. Fabric or flesh, percale or percussive. A drum in the ear is blood pumping. The computer cleaning itself up, speaks of browsing and security optimization. A knee lifts and leans, nudging into the crotchety night. Cheerleaders in aroused cells, their pom-poms, iridescent, whipping the air. Awaken with restart to ensure that automated tune-up modifications take effect. Eros bubbles up, foam on a wave-rise, even in sterile rooms with hard surfaces that resist. What is it about night and nakedness that provokes? The unclothed stroke of time's data, the naked timbre of touch. A stubbed toe on a metal trunk at the end of the bed near the edge of a page—one kind of kiss. Some in need will latch onto anything. He's a twitch-tailed wolf, teeth gleaming. She's foxy and churring in faux fur flung aside, a shadowy reveal, an intent abandoned to its fate.

his deficiency.

Cat-tail *Moss . Isothecium myosuroides*
Common as cats, yes, **purr**-common from sea to middle elevations

An Electric Tightrope

Ready to save her, or is it *savour*, with off-kilter listing, though kilter is safer. It is wise and equilibrial to hold the balance pole near the centre, lessening the thrill factor but edging up certainty when hanging by a strand. When the captor spares the victim, a bond forms and love is possible, an iron-clad loyalty. He's labelled his computer *Hustler*, he fingers it, leans to its face, shifts his chair closer to the table where he sits alone. The passing urban birds stride with high-heel clicks and pressure on the metatarsal. Keeps them on their toes, the current, that is. Some men seem to own the world. This is the time of year to go off to the interior to dip toes and lines and have a measured, ungroomed taste of wilderness. You can get anything if your mortgage or your heart is big enough and with the right fly and knowledge of a lake's structure, and steadiness on the line. Form may have lost most of its steam. Why all the declaratives? "It's a short week," they say around the third day. The cable trembles in the wind, the foot arched and slippered slides forward, locks tension in the upturned jaws. Meanwhile ... at every Brand Name Outlet Special Savings Day or Midnight Madness. There's a daredevil and a saviour drawing eyes and breathing power at each connection to the wire.

meows its way **across** tree branches, **boulders and logs,**
can hang like a long-hair in **strands** from branches
or form **creeping** mats

Her Brancusi Head

An appearance of weight and mass, and white smoothness. A charged memory of shape in the Musée National d'Art Moderne. Is it love or grace that spurs the hankering of hands? Time jiggles air all about. A Zen-master urges presentness, but chill and longing just over the left shoulder beckon attention. For a moment a sense of air's spaciousness and all the molecules of the universe passing through your open body, of its shell-nature of oneness, of your other-than-I-think-I-am-ness. The head there though, a density. Antin speaks of love as language as love. You have to keep gazing and gaping with flow or the plug sets. It's a pugnacious game, jabbed and bounced in words and air. The channel clicked over when blood splattered and pooled—there's a limit. Technology rarely cooperates when most needed. A weight in space that seems a dense mass. The beloved light splay of her hair across your knee, waft of white lilac, nodding green grasses, a kiss of breeze. If only now, what of responsibility, of a tower that soars, a billow's levity, a pillowed weight.

glossy or dingy green.
But its electrified sibling is another matter,
bright and abuzz

Blood On The Wire

Leonard Cohen saw a bird, but now the shape of air and a bend or crimp. Seems from the snags, the wranglers have been through driving their cows against the fence, or something worse. The golden-bean is out, glimmers the slopes with bright yellow flowers amidst rippling grasses. Spring is a wonderful seasoning. Ticks wait in the long grass with hope for a passing animal. Such a fate. He was killed when he stepped on a buried bomb just a few feet from base, the soldier next to him took minor injuries, both so far from home. Why this one, not that one? A matter of inches, of relative irrelevance when a body's density explodes. Sports commentators speak in the language of war, and beauty in motion. A slight vibration as fluid hits fibre. As metal into bone. He can still hear the song humming, electric, in his inner ear. Music, such a reason to live, such a human joy. A morning like no other, filled with warbler song, all that yellow, and once was free of misery.

like **Eric Clapton** when he plugged back in.
Electrified ***cat****-tail moss*
whether or not you're a moss-purist

The Man With A Nosebleed

Tilts his head back to keep life from pouring out. The body keeps its secrets mostly under wraps but occasionally reveals a rupture, a cough, a stumble, in spontaneity a coupling. Red, the most striking. But black's the common wardrobe colour, worn for sombre ceremony, casual attendance, or flung off in a heated moment, and also on steeds that lug and bump, ubiquitous on the circling carousel. With a big whisk she stirs the frappaccino to a froth while Zimmerman honks his nasal tone. The vulnerability of any joint—wrist or ankle, all bones delicate—invites a kiss. The body is an artefact, a museum and somewhere right now it's a plastinated all-too-real-inside-out-revealed husk on display in a gallery in a major city where panes of glass soar high and wide. An icy towel jammed against his nose, in an auto, he reels, races against time. "There's a career here," they often say when they don't mean it, but sometimes they do. How to know? These are the fluids you'll need, especially with the dust. Nothing excites more than a glimpse down a shirt, a nose for trouble. The attendant is petite, alluringly fragile, dressed in white, but not a nurse. Numbers jump in our heads—for instance, nine or eleven, or seventy-seven, a lucky one on a yellow race car, or on Nicole Brossard's white page etched with smart articulating letters. All that ground to cover, and what's ground in on the oval track, on the fingered sheet, on a nostril's breathing edge. A cold white cloth, a heart a-flutter, a breeze's touch, a backward lean, all do make the forehead spin.

it'll get your attention
like Dylan at Newport in '65
wailing with Butterfield blues men

Sleeper With A Whip

Bombed-out horizon but you can't see as far as the crumbled edge. A certain amount of Eros rustles in the packed stuffy room, full of ears, where the river can be glimpsed ululating its glittery slip toward conjunction. A sanctuary against so many troubled names. Forty years in the evolution of pop since Sergeant Pepper and Blondes in the stylus. Words interpreted in the *Daily*. Repressors pretend to be liberators. As suggested the chamber was packed with intelligent minds, the studies far-reaching but little was said of damage, of bruises-never-healed, of numbers-not-reported, though poets always speak from their tiny lofts, their Russias, their walls. Shambles at the edge of perfect lawns. No one sleeps well any longer though snoring is common. Time to apply the nasal-strip, the pesti-herbicide, the sunscreen, the face mask, the rubber glove, the weather tip, the snap-to-attention, the ringed condom, the broadband connection, the HOV lane, the baggage x-ray, the solar kite and the whitening dip. Dark side to a spring morning though marigolds bloom their merry golds and pansies nod with mostly happy faces, but for the dark purple one, almost black. Songs are still alive and elastic in your mind and adrift in the universe. So much professional development and what is learned? Let's buck up and soak up water for the oil in the tar sands. Let's wake and bucket our belongings and move to the promised land just over there across the brambles. That leather tip again bites hard with ambition, gritty in the teeth, and welting the skin.

an electrified "Like a Rolling Stone."
And you know what they say about one of those—
It gathers no ...

Frosting. Her Sex

The eroticism of boats, their curvaceous shape and proximity to water. The rain so steady and a chilly breeze that might wash or blow it all away raises buds of skin and liquid aureoles. Vessels massive, or delicate, slice—with a break of sun, a butterfly, freed from its cocoon, sails the air, awakens visions of sugar plums, fairied escape. You want to put your lips there, you know where, have your cake and eat it too. And who wouldn't, with the statistics on depression published in *Psychology Today*. An adventure waits to be jumped on, or stolen from. Is your life a canoe, a ferry, a freighter? Water rocks. Opalescent eyes flow into your sorrow, her skin's sweet scent stirs hunger, her pale open arms offer rest. One butterfly is an anomaly and endangered, way out here at rest on a coiled mooring rope. Rocks in the water. There is a name for the place where the tide pushes both ways, either way—you can let go or paddle. Through the froth. Drift, avoid the rush to land, where solidity aches your shins. In the rocking, her salt spills, her sugar unfurls, assails, overflows your lifted spoon.

but let it stop and *I-**my**osuroides* waits to pounce.

*Big Red Stem . Pleurosium sch**rebar**i*
Big Red is ready, upright, ascending

Invested In Advertising

Chain or local, local is the choice. He has a cute voice, the five-year old soloist. The athletic shoe fitter has her salt-and-pepper hair cropped extremely short and is as fit or fitter than the proverbial instrument. Television tells you what to need, what to buy. New runners fit like a perfect note from gutty strings rubbed by a Mongolian horsehair bow, but the rain seems indeterminate. A lawyer's affinity for trench coats. Or dick or journalist of the old-school. Which colour is faster, red or neon green? The actor enters the café without on-stage flourish and passes out postcards for the voyage with the title set in red ink. So too the smokestacks. It's a promo, subtle and local. No guitar-play can match the slide of Robert Johnson, no smoke the smoke in his stack. Time soon for the skinfold pinch test, then sip more peppery herb tea, then the phone call to the woman in distress, all raddle, warp and pawl. A tear can flow for miles. Soaked inside, drenched outside, the glassy drops, the glossy message, the subtle sway, the helpless sigh after all words sayable said, the indeterminacy of inevitable purchases.

.

from its interwoven colony.
And how to know its readiness?
By its redness of course, by its

Pushing Against The Road

Every morning a voyage, a ship from port, an unblanketed parrot, steam from the kettle. A Fibonacci kind of day, a hope that things add up, even if erratically. So many metaphors built around the path, its foliage edges. Not yet out of bed, the onset of day seems to press down the shoulders. A yawn's release in the jaw, and the neck relaxes, hands reach out as though ready for the wheel, another metaphor, another circle. Heave up, go with it (or not), the teapot at hand. Pronouns creep in, like chai's spice-sweet aroma. Stairs step, one-at-a-time, to it. The tongue stings for a lingering moment with heat, with heart. A phone call anticipated to lead the way. Asphalt or gravel, filled with juts and holes. The route is always beneath. You and Jack Kerouac and everyone reacted against the A-bomb that lingers still, in the fiery sky in every dark descent, whether pressed back with countdown or tilted toward, ready, latent flash seen in a squint through the bug-splattered screen, whether everyone knows or not. Flick the switch and struggle up. Departure is imminent, the seconds click, then rocket.

blunt leafy habit.
But could it be a rouge ruse feigned?
A posture made in a shortage of

The Dewy Lumber

The street is picturesque, its own wilderness. So many flashes give
evidence of our existence through a lens of decimals. Eternity in an
Infiniti ad signals and turns left with the advanced green. Banks adjust
for the unanticipated pressure to raise interest rates and trees are a
commodity just like everything. If only the dead artists could collect
from the auction house. An Elvis wave in an Adidas track suit slack
against a trunk. Dress styles return to the sack and the empire waist-
line. In a few seconds they're tossed over the head, a shape is disguised
as time unnoticed passes, mysteriously still sexy. It's not a story but is
interrupted by family obligations, hanging reverse curls and crunches on
the ball. Beads of sweat can be a demonstration of virility, a turn-on. The
left side sags, collapses with pain. It's always win or lose, even when you're
overdressed or in the library's spine-stack number game. Athletic vocal
chords bellow an expletive with erupting decibels. Your arms feel like
rubber after holding forearm-plank position for three minutes even with
the moisture in the air and the gracious beauty of the teacher. When the
chainsaws come out you can bet someone weeps.

males—a sexual crisis? After all, it
cannot reproduce—asexually—as they say.
And who'd want to anyway, given a choice.

Fierce Emergence

A low place, marshy, pretends to be the end of things, but on closer study, a foot-soaking look, new life is vivid. The shining eye, the burning eye, zest and contrition. One of—how many—species: vole, moose, rhino, redstart, starfish, snail, rainbow trout—the list goes on forever—well scratch the rhino in this hemisphere—or two if the ark is ready. This morning pain, ache in a muscle newly worked. So many questions of continuance. Should you come out? Go on—off? Love warms the world (they say), whether red chili-pepper love, ice-pack love, love among ferns, or barbed wire. Can't keep up, despite exponential growth in the use of cement, steel and cheapest labour. The tight clasp-dance of clerics and Mafioso. The concrete sets up and soon a structure will rise, and a pepper-plant and a penis, the pepper with multiple imitation red phalli. Where is love today if you take its temperature? Around the eyes, flesh feels thick, laden with the unsaid, like alligator skin. Dandelions, plague, or cleansing vegetable-green, or essence of a pale wine. Piercing eyes spark the moment's tinder veneer.

It remains robust, ***hopeful*** you might say, nonetheless

*Rough Moss . Claopodium **crisp**ifolium*
As with many, a moss of **humility**, shown

Your Head Like The Lemon

Morning brain, grogged, morning rain a threat, yet showers a soft surprise on crusty streets. An orchard and a mine and a lover-once-loved passes by a window. Tumescent with feeling; turmeric for the inflammation. Dig into the core of it or go softly with the probe of observation. Extract the lie or truth of it to expunge. David Crosby sang the national anthem at the hockey finale and "Love the One You're With" or was that Stephen Stills—and did he? Doubt fills and answers are hollows. Though *no love's lost* (which means its opposite) when the ice sets and the puck drops. Fame and memory blend to confuse. A straw sheath floats to the gritty ground and settles to point in a direction that gives no clue. A wheat field at the edge of town bobs and ripples and *golden* is the usual adjective, but the wheat is truly more pale, paler than citrus skin or a fright-night double-header. From the mine's dirty depth may come a shimmery glint, a mustard-yellow puff or the blackest of blacks. A lover appears stern in the set of her eyes, until lowered. The mantle is stippled and fractures. Acidic zest's involuntary pucker.

by the down-turned head
this one a citizen of logs and tree bases.
A moss with heart-shaped leaves.

Envying Lilies

Their perky beauty. An evening of airplanes and baseball. Lives lived in shards of attention, many-shaped, many-coloured, many-edged. A line drive and a sharp take-off around the diamond. So complacent, yet impatient, in the game, for there's always one better. A skin-tag on a cuticle resists searching teeth. Scheduled and scheduled again for convenience, possibility, and still dropped despite the absence of rain—what's to do? Is it not a sin, even when harmless (but who defines the sin)? Everything left behind but the self and several others and a few conveniences in the steep penetration of clouds. Clench teeth and fiddle skin to ease anxiety. They were yellow and prolific, bobbing. A winner is announced—the best poet, the best bloom! Are you among them, either one? It was a bases-loaded cakewalk, the safest landing and graceful at that. We are flowering and inured, floundering and easily annoyed, petalled and metallic.

Gazing down the heart is discovered
straight and spreading when graced with moisture's plenishment
and contorted and upright when dry.

Indexed And Written

In a roundabout way Adam Dickinson makes a case for taxonomy in *Kingdom, Phylum*. Can you say *nouning* the way you can say *writing*? Depends on the mat you stand on. Dance is in the offing, and rolls over a bar set near shoulder-height. The television quiz show is a narrative of profit and loss, an economic structure deeper that the pixillated screen and perpetuated. How many realities live in a day or dance on the head of a pin? Sand is annoyance in the shoe and many books open. Words narrow, but like wrist-binding can excite the bed. If you say it's so you make it so. 'Soso' is a pseudonym for a hip-hop artist from Saskatoon named Troy Gronsdahl. Those stairs painted black again but scuffed so the white shows through and up, to interruption. Suddenly a bear and an unpaid invoice, all feral. Does a wild animal recognize a *corridor*, man-made with green trees and low round rocks? The aged gentleman lowers tentatively into the barber chair. It is habit more than necessity, the hair diminishing, the poem poeming, a pomade on reality. Sing the alphabetized categories while sliding open the small narrow doors of the card catalogue, soon to be antiqued. It's a key-word world and you're whirled—and the answer is yes.

Sometimes *Claopodium* likes it rough,
a bit of danger and abrasion,
but with a look deeper in to leaf cells

91

A Peak, A Pear

All morning relatives were rising and shining—or not—still tired. Last night, veils and voluptuous flesh swooshed and shimmied the room, sequins a-shimmer. Swords and bangles. Today a scatter of chairs and up and down stairs to the pills and the postal box. The seeds of the real task hidden beneath Bosch skin and fibrous flesh. Yoshimasu Gōzō writes of the double mountain, or red and green, so beautiful. The themes of the dances were found in Egypt, Persia, Sevilla and Las Vegas, but were all spirit. *La morte nature* only gets you so far and a word flips on a *kay* and an *ahr*. The current pressing to paper is a strange experience, all glittery eyelashes, a milky lake and misreading *thing* as *thigh*. The pill-ration sorted out, the wish for an end to chronic pain in the left arm, the question of the cell-phone service. Dance bobs up and transports. Fruity globes bob to the surface, even seeds afloat in disconnected limbo. And were beautiful hips and hands mentioned, hips bumping toward you, hands curling gracefully in air? You fall speechless in the key light or the afterglow. You know you're weaker when the precious orb slips from your hands and tumbles, down, down, toward a bruise.

the humble one **discovers**
diamonds
among the regularly **feathery** (once-pinnate) **shades**

Everything Appears To Shine

A murmur of rumours and truths and how to net the necessary-to-know, to turn from scared to sacred. There are models for letting it all in, or as much as is graspable in the fleeting. Trucks with scrapers and brushes scour the street, gouge and push winter debris. The beauty of the car-less way arched in memory with trees in summer greens. Some days seem a rock-scissors-paper game, a dream of flashing hands and domination or surrender. Some days, all words, their tiny strokes. Where is the plastic health card, and where are Robert Kelly and Elizabeth Willis when you need them? Coffee mug left behind with the homeopath. You recall a yellow blossom, a dead tree and a poppy plant mistaken for a weed. Everything spins and everyone is on top or not. Glimmer of life seen from outer space, all fossil fuels and television. Green tea cools in the white cup. Sun, though hard to believe in the still-chilly wane of winter, will warm. On her cheek, on his brow, a secret is revealed, a gleam that speaks. Hands in air, across a gap, along an upholstered seam, propelled by particular light, by something felt, recalled, by not so much as a word, but a smile—by deity, karma, fate, by murmurs, the sweep, the dazzle, the thirst.

lime, olive, and yellow—that **edgy spectrum** of green
along a stream or **wherever**
a light-gap

opens.

A Note on the Titles and Other Acknowledgements

Several years ago, fellow poet and collaborator Hilary Clark introduced me to the work of the American poet Elizabeth Willis via her book *Meteoric Flowers* (Wesleyan University Press, 2006) which I found to be a gem. Then I read Willis' earlier book *Turneresque* (Burning Deck, 2003). These works spoke to me and led me out of a lull and into a new work that became what you read here.

I took a few words from the text in Willis' first poem in *Meteoric Flowers* as the title to generate my own poem. This became a compelling force, driving the poem, and so I continued to do so with each of her poems in the two books mentioned. I took her words as my title and catalyst, then began to shape my own poem. I resisted taking her most lovely and elegant and complete phrases, because I did not want to co-opt her creations. Instead I took words beside each other, but that often lacked 'completeness' as a phrase. I must say, they have come to make complete sense and lose their oddity as I have lived with them for so long now. The result is the eighty-nine pieces included here. Thank you, Elizabeth Willis.

Thank you to the 'Crackers' poetry group I was part of in Saskatoon, and my friends there—Hilary Clark, Jennifer Still, Mari-Lou Rowley—whose early encouragement with this direction prompted me to carry on. I am most grateful to Fred Wah, whose acute eye and astute questions guided the final editorial process.

Thank you to the editors of the following publications who have presented versions of some of these poems: *Grain Magazine*, *Dandelion*, *filling station*, and *The Spoken Word Workbook: Inspiration from Poets Who Teach*.

I also want to acknowledge: the Saskatchewan Arts Board which provided a grant to develop these pieces; writer and friend Carolynn Hoy and Willowbend for providing a retreat place and time; Galiano Island where I really began to look at moss; the Leighton Colony at The Banff Centre where I did the penultimate polish on this work; and to Galiano Island again, for a final tuning of the work, and winter walks among the drenched, turned-out, turned-on mosses.

Phrases from Elizabeth Willis' work are used by permission of the author and of Wesleyan University Press (*Meteoric Flowers*) and Burning Deck Press (*Turneresque*).

—Steven Ross Smith